VEGETARIAN GRUB ON A GRANT

Cas Clarke wrote her first book, *Grub on a Grant*, after taking a degree in Urban Studies at Sussex University. She now lives in a rural retreat in Surrey with her husband Andy, son James, daughter Helena and their mad cat and dog, Matti and Barney.

Nicole,
Happy
Christmas
Love from
Jo + Mark
xxxx

Vegetarian Grub on a Grant

Cas Clarke

HEADLINE

First published in 1996
by HEADLINE BOOK PUBLISHING

10 9 8 7 6 5 4 3 2

Illustrations by Mike Gordon

ISBN 0 7472 5204 1

Typeset by
Letterpart Limited, Reigate, Surrey

Printed and bound in Great Britain by
Cox & Wyman Ltd, Reading, Berks

HEADLINE BOOK PUBLISHING
A division of Hodder Headline PLC
338 Euston Road
London NW1 3BH

To my darling Andy, James and Helena.

Raw eggs

The Department of Health advises that babies, elderly people, those pregnant or ill should not eat dishes – for example hollandaise sauce or meringues – containing raw eggs but that any eggs should be thoroughly cooked until both the yolk and white are solid. For other people there is very little risk from eating eggs cooked by any method; raw eggs, however, are not advised.

Contents

Introduction

It took me a long time but at last I have finally got around to doing a veggie version of *Grub on a Grant*. The problem with most cookery books for students is that they don't take into account the real problems students have to cope with. The obvious one is lack of money, but the problems don't end there. Many students have no real experience of cooking for themselves (which often leads to a lack of confidence in their abilities as a cook) and many suffer from lack of space and facilities for cooking. Add to that the demands of shopping and the problems of storage (and people 'borrowing' your food) and you begin to get some idea of what most students are up against.

I didn't want to fall into the trap of producing a book which wasn't relevant to student needs – and it's a good few years since I was a student! So, when I decided to write this book (which many people have asked for) the first thing I did was go through my cupboards and chuck out all my food stores. Then I drew up a list of all the ingredients that I relied on in my student days: e.g. cans of beans, tomatoes and sweetcorn; the vegetables used most often, such as onions, garlic, mushrooms and peppers; a few store cupboard ingredients, such as packets of rice, pasta and lentils; finally, some cheese, eggs, margarine, milk and bread – and I had the basic student diet. These are the ingredients that these recipes are based on. Other vegetables do appear – potatoes, courgettes, carrots, aubergines, broccoli, cauliflower, even fresh herbs! But these are always bought with a specific recipe in mind.

I then relegated the food processor, liquidiser and assorted kitchen gadgets to the back of the deepest cupboards. Armed only with the basics that students usually have: a sharp knife (yes, I allowed myself the luxury of a *sharp* knife – but you could keep it in your room), a tin opener, a wooden spoon, two saucepans, a frying pan, a baking tray and a casserole dish, I felt ready to start.

I now have the luxury of a dishwasher, while most students have to wash their utensils. No, sorry! *First* they have to find their utensils under the mound of unwashed dishes in the sink and wash them before they can start cooking.

As the months rolled by I hunted out the garlic crusher and the cheese grater (muttering that some students do have these items) and life got easier. Occasionally I used pastry and conscientiously rolled it out with a milk bottle. Then a worrying thought occurred to me: many people now buy their milk in cartons! I managed to flatten the pastry into my dish – not a brilliant solution but it was adequate.

At long last, as my deadline approached and I cooked the last recipe, I breathed a sigh of relief. Looking through these pages I was happy that the recipes lived up to the goals that I had set myself. All of them are simple to prepare and certainly will not make too big a hole in the budget. A few from the original *Grub on a Grant*, ones that have stood the test of time, reappear, as do one or two from some of my other books. Two that spring to mind are Passion Cake and Mean Beans which have been very popular.

I hope that you will enjoy this book and that soon you will be producing your own culinary masterpieces!

Items to take to college

Essential

knife
tin opener
wooden spoon
cutlery and crockery
tea-towel
one-person casserole dish

small saucepan
large saucepan with lid
frying pan
baking tray
chopping board

Really useful

colander or sieve
measuring spoons and jug
mixing bowl
whisk
cheese grater
garlic press
20-cm (8-in) flan tin – for pastry dishes and some sweet
    dishes
corkscrew

For cooking with friends
large casserole dish
lasagne dish
a second large saucepan

Basic store cupboard

coffee
tea
sugar (if used)
milk (if used)   Essential to get you through
margarine/butter   your first night/morning
eggs and/or cheese   before the shops open
bread

The ideal parents would also supply

dried bean mix   balti paste
rice   mango chutney
pasta   tomato purée
cornflour   vegetable stock cubes
split red lentils   mixed herbs
breakfast cereal   oregano
Marmite   salt and pepper
peanut butter   can chick peas
tomato ketchup   can baked beans
soy sauce   can sweetcorn
oil   can chopped tomatoes

And some fresh vegetables to start you off

potatoes   mushrooms
onions   tomatoes
green pepper   carrots
garlic   courgettes

Handy hints

- Read the recipe *carefully* to ensure you understand it. Please pay attention to words such as 'gently simmer' – this means just that. If you go ahead and boil it, you will end up with a burnt pan and dried-up food! Also watch out for grilling on a 'medium' heat. Again, if you grill on high, you will probably end up with a burnt offering, or worse, a flash fire.

- Ovens vary enormously, but you will soon learn how yours behaves. If dishes start coming out overdone, turn the heat down by 10°C/25°F/Gas 1 whenever you cook; on the other hand, if dishes always take longer to cook than the recipe states, turn the heat up by the same amount.

- The measures in all the recipes are approximate; nothing will go dreadfully wrong if you use slightly more or less of an ingredient than stated in the recipe. If you do not have a tablespoon you can use a teaspoon for your measuring: 3 teaspoons = 1 tablespoon.

- Quantities of seasonings are only given as a guide. You will soon learn to adjust them to your taste. *Warning*: if, for example, you are cooking a hot dish for the first time for friends, for example, curry or chilli sin carne, *check first* whether they like it hot or mild. It is too late after you have added the chilli powder.

- I have used some fresh herbs in these recipes – mainly basil and coriander. The taste they give a dish is completely different from that of dried herbs. If you cannot obtain them try substituting parsley or mint.

- Some recipes use canned pulses, such as kidney beans, butter beans, chick peas, etc. It is much cheaper if you buy them dry, allow them to soak and boil them yourself. The catch is that you have to remember to soak them overnight and they do take a while to cook.

For those of you who want to save those extra pennies, here is the method. The weight of the dried beans is half that of the cooked beans, so only half the amount stated in the recipe is needed. Soak the beans overnight. Drain and boil in fresh water for 10 minutes. Simmer for 1–1½ hours or until the beans are soft. (If you have forgotten to soak the beans, boil them for 10 minutes, turn off the heat, cover and leave to soak for 1 hour.) *Do not* add any seasoning at this point as this lengthens the cooking time. Cook the beans as directed in the recipe.

Some beans do not require such a long cooking time and these are pointed out in individual recipes. Lentils need no preparation: just use as directed in the recipes.

- When heating up yoghurt, do so *very* gently or it will separate.

- If you do not use all the contents of a can at once, do not keep the remainder in the can. Transfer it to a plastic or china bowl. If left in the can, the contents can develop a metallic taste.

- Make sure you have some foil or clingfilm for wrapping any leftover or unused vegetables, for example, peppers or onions. Store them, if possible, in a refrigerator.

- Items often go missing from communal refrigerators. Prime targets are milk, butter and cheese. Sometimes casual thieves are deterred if you keep your foodstuffs in a plastic box with your name on it. This, however, will not deter the professional thief – you just have to be lucky to catch them. *Never* let them go if you are lucky enough to catch one – they will only consider you a *sucker* and continue stealing.

- Be enterprising when cooking. If you do not have the exact pan or dish that the recipe states, substitute with a similar dish. However, do be careful about checking whether dishes are flame-proof. I lost three casserole dishes at college through friends either trying to use them on direct heat or putting the hot dishes into cold water. It is better to let the dishes cool gradually.

- If you are lucky enough to be given, or are able to buy, a toasting machine, this can be very handy for making a breakfast or lunch snack. Most machines come with a recipe book. Our favourites were cheese and pickle or baked-bean sandwiches. Sweet toasted sandwiches can also be made with banana or apple. Toasted sandwiches are quick and easy to make and very filling. My friend Sue and I virtually lived off them one summer until my mother noticed her toasting machine had disappeared from home.

- Where a recipe states serve with rice or pasta, allow 50–75 g (2–3 oz) dry weight per person. Allow approximately 150–200 g (6–8 oz) bought weight or 50 g (2 oz) frozen vegetables per person.

- Where quantities are given for dinner parties the dish serves the stated number of people as part of a set menu.

The symbols found opposite certain recipes indicate:

- ❂   this recipe uses only one dish during preparation

- ◷   this recipe can be made in half an hour or less

1 The Quick Snack

As students are often in a hurry when it comes to preparing meals, it is important to have a range of snacks that can be quickly put together. In fact, the diet of many students consists of snacks, snacks and more snacks! If you are not to fall into the trap of living off takeaways and processed foods (expensive and not particularly healthy), this is certainly a good chapter to get to grips with.

A big favourite with students is things on toast. However, as sometimes you may have to share one small grill with a large number of other students (often all trying to cook at the same time), it helps if you have a few other dishes that you can resort to if the queue for the grill looks too long for the time you have available.

Don't forget that if you can find time in the morning to prepare some sandwiches or filled rolls to take for your lunch, this is a good way of saving money. However, this only applies if you then actually eat them! If you end up going with friends to the canteen you will have paid for lunch twice.

Just a qui k word of warning on health. If you find yourself living mainly on snacks, it becomes even more important to include plenty of fruit in your diet. This is not difficult as a piece of fruit is a ready packaged snack. There is only so long the human body can take being stuffed with chips, crisps, pastry, biscuits and chocolate before it rebels with spots, obesity, etc. The choice is yours . . .

Porridge

Serves 1

The time it takes to cook the porridge will depend on the type of porridge oats you use – check the packet instructions.

50 g (2 oz) porridge oats
250 ml (10 fl oz) milk
pinch salt
knob of butter (to serve)
brown sugar (to serve)

Put the oats, milk and salt in a saucepan and cook according to the packet instructions, stirring until you have a creamy consistency. Pour into a bowl, top with a knob of butter and a sprinkling of brown sugar.

Sandwiches

I've given you some of my favourite recipes for sandwiches here, but the main advantage of sandwiches is their endless variety. You can ring the changes with the many different types of bread or rolls now available. Other options to consider are pitta bread, which is very good stuffed, or chappatis, in which you can roll up different fillings.

Suggestions for fillings:
cheese with mayo and corn
cheese and pickle (vary the type of pickle)
cheese with cucumber or tomatoes
soft cream cheese with chopped celery and mayo
hard-boiled egg with Marmite or chopped onion
hard-boiled egg with curry-flavoured mayo
chilli or bean spread with lettuce and/or cucumber
mashed beans with a little of your favourite salad
    dressing
peanut butter and jam (an American favourite)

Beansprouts with hummus sandwich
Serves 1

    2 slices bread
    margarine to spread
    1 tablespoon (15 ml) hummus
    2 tablespoons (30 ml) fresh beansprouts

Spread bread with margarine. Spread 1 slice with hummus, top with beansprouts and then the remaining slice of bread. Serve within 30 minutes of making.

Brie and grape sandwich
Serves 1

    2 slices bread
    margarine to spread
    25 g (1 oz) brie, sliced thinly
    3–4 grapes, halved

Spread bread with margarine. Place cheese on one slice of bread, add grapes and top with the other slice of bread.

Peanut butter and banana sandwich
Serves 1

    2 slices bread
    margarine to spread
    2–3 teaspoons (10–15 ml) peanut butter
    1 small banana, mashed roughly

Spread bread with margarine. Spread one slice with the peanut butter and then with the mashed banana. Top with the remaining slice of bread.

Salad sandwich
Serves 1

2 slices bread, or 1 pitta bread, split
2 teaspoons (10 ml) salad dressing
1 tomato, sliced
few slices cucumber
1 lettuce leaf

Spread both slices of bread with the salad dressing. Put the vegetables on one slice, then top with the other. If using pitta bread, stuff with vegetables and spoon in salad dressing.

Stuffed pitta bread
Serves 1

1 pitta bread, split
50 g (2 oz) feta cheese, sliced
1 tomato, sliced
1 teaspoon (5 ml) oil
1 teaspoon (5 ml) tomato purée

Stuff the pitta bread with the feta cheese and tomato. Mix the oil and tomato purée and spoon into the pitta bread.

Toasted cheese
Serves 1

This is probably the most popular remedy for those late night munchies.

> 2 slices bread
> 50 g (2 oz) cheese
> 2 teaspoons (10 ml) soft margarine
> 1 teaspoon (5 ml) French mustard

Pre-heat the grill. Toast the bread on one side. Turn it over and toast the other side until it crisps but hasn't turned brown. Mash the cheese, margarine and mustard together and spread over the toast. Grill for about 2 minutes until bubbling and starting to brown.

Toasted cheese and tomato
As above, but add 2 teaspoons (10 ml) tomato purée to the cheese mixture before toasting.

Toasted cheese and pickle
As in main recipe, but add 2 teaspoons (10 ml) of your favourite pickle to the cheese mixture before toasting.

Cheese and mango toasties
Serves 1

This is my current version of a cheese and pickle toasted sandwich. You can vary this recipe by using different pickles or chutneys.

> 2 slices bread
> 25 g (1 oz) cheese
> 1 teaspoon (5 ml) soft margarine
> 2 teaspoons (10 ml) mango chutney

Pre-heat the grill. Toast the bread slices on one side only. Meanwhile, mash together the cheese, margarine and mango chutney. Spread this mixture over one of the toasted slices of bread, top with the other slice, untoasted side up. Return to the grill and toast until brown. Turn the toastie over and brown the last untoasted side.

French bread pizza
Serves 1–2

> 1 French baguette, split
> 2 tablespoons (30 ml) tomato purée
> sprinkling oregano
> 50 g (2 oz) cheese, grated
> 2 tomatoes, sliced
> black pepper

Pre-heat the grill. Spread the tomato purée over the cut surfaces of the baguette. Sprinkle with the oregano and the cheese. Top with slices of tomato and season with black pepper. Grill for about 2 minutes until the cheese has melted and is beginning to bubble.

Fried bread
Serves 1

> 1 tablespoon (15 ml) oil
> 1 slice bread, halved

Heat the oil in a pan until very hot, add the bread and immediately turn it over. This ensures that both sides of the bread get coated with oil. Continue to cook, turning as necessary until bot.. sides are crisp and brown. Serve with baked beans, fried eggs, tomatoes or mushrooms.

Carrot and lentil pâté
Serves 2–4

This is a very useful pâté which you can serve with French bread and salad as a lunch dish for 2 people or as a starter for 4.

> 100 g (4 oz) split red lentils
> 100 g (4 oz) carrots, grated
> 1 onion, chopped
> 2 cloves garlic, crushed
> 1 tablespoon (15 ml) oil
> grated rind and juice of ½ lemon
> 1 teaspoon (5 ml) dried thyme
> 25 g (1 oz) butter
> salt and pepper

Cook the lentils in boiling water for 10 minutes, add the carrots, cover and simmer for a further 10 minutes. Fry the onion and garlic in the oil for 5 minutes, then add the lemon juice and rind and the thyme. Continue to cook for 3 minutes. Drain the lentil mixture thoroughly, beat in the butter. Mix everything together and season well. Chill for 1 hour before using.

Spicy cheese and nut pâté
Serves 1

For the days when you want a change from a cheese sandwich or cheese and biscuits lunch, this is ideal. It makes a really delicious quick lunch with French bread or pitta bread.

> 21 g cube of Danish Blue cheese
> 16 g cube of Boursin with garlic and herbs
> 1 tablespoon (15 ml) soft margarine
> 15–25 g Tobago Chilli flavoured roasted peanuts,
>   crushed or roughly chopped

Mash together the cheeses and margarine. Stir in the peanuts and mix well.

Scrambled eggs
Serves 1

> 2 eggs, beaten
> 1 tablespoon (15 ml) milk
> salt and pepper
> 1 tablespoon (15 ml) soft margarine

Beat the eggs and milk together. Season. Melt the margarine in a small saucepan and add the egg mixture. Stir over a low heat for 1–2 minutes until the eggs are set to your taste. (Don't forget that they continue to cook a little after you take them off the heat.)

Cheesy scrambled eggs
When you pour the egg and milk mixture into the pan add 25 g (1 oz) grated cheese.

Savoury scrambled eggs
Serves 1

> 3 spring onions, chopped
> knob of butter
> 2 eggs, beaten
> 1 tablespoon (15 ml) milk
> ¼ teaspoon (1.25 ml) Marmite
> pepper

Cook the onions in the butter in a small frying pan for 1 minute. Beat together the eggs, milk and Marmite. Pour into pan and cook, stirring, for 1–2 minutes until egg has set to a creamy consistency. Serve with buttered toast.

Huevos rancheros ☾
Serves 1

This is very quick and easy to make and always popular for breakfast or lunch. If you have some coriander (either fresh or dried) you could add a little for a really authentic taste. You could also serve it with some oven chips for a tasty supper.

> 230-g can chopped tomatoes
> chilli sauce *or* powder to taste
> 2 eggs
> oil for frying

In a small saucepan heat the tomatoes gently for 10 minutes, until reduced to a sauce. Add chilli to taste. Cover the bottom of a frying pan with oil and heat. Gently break in the eggs. Baste with oil until the yolks become opaque. Spoon sauce on to a plate and arrange eggs on top.

Egg, tomato and mushroom fry-up ✿☾
Serves 1

> 100 g (4 oz) button mushrooms
> 1 tomato, quartered lengthways
> knob of butter
> 1 tablespoon (15 ml) oil
> 1 egg
> salt and pepper

Cook the mushrooms and tomato in the butter for 3–4 minutes. Push to one side of the pan, add the oil and, when it is hot, break the egg carefully into the pan. Season with salt and pepper. Baste the egg with the hot oil until cooked, then serve immediately.

Boiled eggs and Marmite soldiers
Serves 1

There are some who think that recipes for boiled eggs or for baked beans on toast are unnecessary. Perhaps they are unaware of the novice cooks who have tried to cook beans without first removing them from the tin or who have tried to fry onions, whole and without first peeling them! It's difficult to decide just how much detail to go into but I like to think that if you have made it to uni in the first place, you must have some intelligence and common sense.

> 2 eggs
> 2 slices bread
> margarine
> Marmite

Boil some water in a saucepan. Add the eggs carefully and boil for 4 minutes. Toast the bread and spread with margarine and Marmite. Cut each slice into 5 lengths and serve with the boiled eggs.

Baked beans on toast
Serves 1

> 200–400-g can baked beans (depending on appetite!)
> 2 slices bread
> margarine

Toast the bread while warming the beans in a small saucepan. Spread the toast with margarine and top with beans. Grated cheese or chilli sauce can be added to vary this feast.

The alternative beans on toast
Serves 1

½ 430-g can chilli beans
2 petits pains rolls or 20-cm (8-in) French baguette
25 g (1 oz) cheese, grated

Pre-heat the grill. In a small saucepan heat the beans. Do not boil. Split open the rolls or baguette and place on a heat-proof tray. Pile beans on to bread, sprinkle with cheese and grill for 2–3 minutes, until the cheese has melted and is bubbling.

Fried potatoes
Serves 1

75 g (3 oz) potatoes, peeled and cubed
1 tablespoon (15 ml) oil
salt and pepper

Mix the potatoes and oil in a bowl and season well. Heat a frying pan until hot, add the oil covered potatoes and fry until brown on all sides. This should take about 6–10 minutes, depending on the size of your potato cubes.

2 Cooking for One

In your first term (or maybe even your first year) at uni, the chances are that whether you live in hall, a student flat or a bedsit, the cooking you do will usually be for one. Later on you will probably find friends that you can share the cooking with at least some of the time.

It's a well-known fact that many people, faced with cooking for one, just don't bother. But . . . it is a good way of saving money and it's better for your diet than continually living off processed food. (Look at the ingredients next time you buy a ready made meal – do you really want all those additives?) There are many meals for one that can be cooked in minutes and are really very easy to prepare. At the beginning of term being busy in the kitchen is a great way of meeting people and making new friends. (Fifteen years on, two of my best friends are people I shared a kitchen with that first year.) So even if you haven't had a great deal to do with the kitchen up until now, this is the time to get to grips with its pleasures!

Mexican bean soup

Serves 1

This is a really easy soup to make and is a great supper dish. You can also make it with beans in chilli sauce. A small portion would be a delicious starter for a Mexican meal.

1 small onion, chopped
1 small green pepper, diced
1 tablespoon (15 ml) oil
225-g can beans in spicy sauce
225-g can chopped tomatoes
tortilla chips (to serve)
grated cheese (to serve)

In a small saucepan, fry the onion and pepper in the oil for 10 minutes until soft and starting to brown. Add the beans and tomatoes and stir well. Simmer gently for 10–15 minutes. Serve topped with tortilla chips and grated cheese.

Provençale salad
Serves 1

You can of course use ordinary tomatoes for this recipe, but I prefer 'beef' tomatoes (the big slicing variety). You could also use just one type of pepper instead of the two I have – but using two adds to the colourfulness of this dish.

1 egg
½ red pepper
½ green pepper
1 courgette, grated
1 'beef' tomato, sliced
few slices red onion
25 g (1 oz) black pitted olives, halved

Dressing
1 tablespoon (15 ml) tomato purée
1 tablespoon (15 ml) oil
1 teaspoon (5 ml) wine vinegar
1 clove garlic, crushed
salt and pepper

Boil the egg for 10 minutes and then leave to cool. Pre-heat the grill. Cut each pepper in half, grill, skin side up, until skin blackens, then cut into strips. Shell the boiled egg and cut into wedges. Arrange the salad ingredients on a plate. Mix together all the dressing ingredients and drizzle over salad.

Spicy Chinese salad

Serves 1

100 g (4 oz) fresh beansprouts
2 Chinese cabbage leaves, chopped
100 g (4 oz) canned sweetcorn
½ red pepper, diced
2 spring onions, chopped
2 celery sticks, chopped

Dressing
1 tablespoon (15 ml) tomato purée *or* ketchup
1 tablespoon (15 ml) wine vinegar
1 tablespoon (15 ml) soy sauce
2 tablespoons (30 ml) orange juice
½ teaspoon (2.5 ml) ginger purée

Mix all salad ingredients together. Now mix all dressing ingredients together and pour over the salad.

Hulu Hoops salad

Serves 1

This is a really crunchy salad that makes an ideal lunch dish –
but prepare it at the last minute or the Hulu Hoops will go soft.

½ 198-g can sweetcorn, drained
2 sticks celery, sliced
2 tomatoes, sliced *or* 6 cherry tomatoes
30-g packet original Hulu Hoops

Dressing
2 tablespoons (30 ml) cheese and chive spread
1 tablespoon (15 ml) natural yoghurt

Put all salad ingredients in a serving bowl. Beat together the
cheese and chive spread and the yoghurt until smooth. Dress
the salad and serve immediately.

Carrot salad

Serves 1

An easy side salad that goes with most dishes – I particularly like it with curries.

100 g (4 oz) carrots, grated

Dressing
1 tablespoon (15 ml) oil
1 tablespoon (15 ml) orange juice
1 teaspoon (5 ml) wholegrain mustard
1 teaspoon (5 ml) white wine vinegar

Mix all dressing ingredients together and pour over the grated carrot. Serve.

Tomato, cheese and courgette salad

Serves 1

2 large tomatoes
1 courgette, grated
50 g (2 oz) cheese, sliced

Dressing
1 tablespoon (15 ml) oil
1 tablespoon (15 ml) tomato ketchup
salt and pepper

Dice one tomato, mix with courgette and place on a serving plate. Slice the other tomato. Cover the courgette and diced tomato mixture with slices of cheese and tomato. Mix together the dressing ingredients and spoon over salad. Serve.

Mexican salad ◔

Serves 1

    1 avocado, peeled, stoned and halved
    pinch coriander
    2 tomatoes, sliced
    ½ 200-g can red kidney beans, drained
    few slices red onion
    1 tablespoon (15 ml) tomato purée
    1 tablespoon (15 ml) oil
    1 teaspoon (5 ml) wine vinegar
    few drops chilli sauce

Thinly slice one half of the avocado on to a plate. Roughly mash the other half and mix with the coriander. Place this on your plate, and beside it put the sliced tomatoes. Now mix the remaining ingredients and scatter over the avocado and tomatoes. Serve immediately.

Veggie varsity pie ✷◔

Serves 1

When *Grub on a Grant* was first published my Varsity Pie was one of the first recipes to prove popular. Therefore I felt I really ought to include a veggie version in this book.

    125-g can condensed mushroom soup
    100-g can sweetcorn
    100-g can beans
    2 slices wholemeal bread, buttered
    25 g (1 oz) cheese, grated

Pre-heat the oven to 190°C/375°F/Gas 5. Mix together the soup, sweetcorn and beans and put into a small casserole dish. Halve the bread and place, buttered side up, on top of the mixture. Sprinkle with the grated cheese and bake for 25 minutes.

Undone pie
Serves 1

125-g can condensed vegetable soup
200-g can baked beans
1 tablespoon (15 ml) tomato purée
1 tomato, sliced
2 thick slices French bread, buttered
50 g (2 oz) cheese, grated

Pre-heat the oven to 180°C/350°F/Gas 4. Mix the soup, beans and tomato purée together. Arrange the tomato slices in the bottom of a small ovenproof dish. Cover with the soup mixture. Cut the bread slices in half and use to top dish. Sprinkle with cheese and bake for 25 minutes.

Butter bean bake
Serves 1

200-g can butter beans
125-g can condensed mushroom soup
1–2 slices wholemeal bread, buttered
25 g (1 oz) cheese, grated

Pre-heat the oven to 180°C/350°F/Gas 4. Put the beans and soup into a small casserole dish. Cut the bread slices in half and arrange them, buttered side up, over the top. Sprinkle with the cheese and bake for 25 minutes.

Vegetarian bolognese bake ⚙

Serves 1

  1 portion vegetarian bolognese sauce (see page 35)
  1 tomato, thinly sliced
  25 g (1 oz) cheese, grated
  200 g (8 oz) baked potato, sliced
  melted butter *or* margarine

Pre-heat the oven to 200°C/400°F/Gas 6. Place the bolognese sauce in a casserole dish and cover with the sliced tomato and cheese. Arrange the potato slices on top and brush with melted butter or margarine. Bake for 30 minutes.

Curried bean crumble ◔

Serves 1

  1 onion, diced
  ½ green pepper, diced
  1 tablespoon (15 ml) oil
  200-g can curried beans
  2 slices wholemeal bread, crumbed
  25 g (1 oz) cheese, grated

Pre-heat the grill. Fry the onion and pepper in the oil until soft. Add the beans and heat gently. Transfer to a flame-proof dish. Mix together the breadcrumbs and cheese and sprinkle over the vegetables. Grill until the cheese melts. Serve immediately.

Bean bangers

Serves 1

These are very tasty and extremely easy to make. Use plenty of crumbs to coat and shape the bangers *gently*.

200-g can barbecue beans, drained, reserving the sauce
2 slices bread, crusts removed and crumbed
dried wholemeal crumbs for coating
oil for frying

Mash the beans and mix with the fresh breadcrumbs. Divide the mixture into four, and carefully shape into four small sausages (fat and thick rather than long and thin). Put plenty of dried crumbs on a plate. Roll the sausages in the crumbs, patting into all sides. Put enough oil in a small frying pan to just cover the bottom. Heat it and fry the bangers for 3–4 minutes until brown all over. Meanwhile, heat the reserved barbecue sauce gently in a small pan; serve with bean bangers.

Baked cheese sandwich

Serves 1

2 slices bread, buttered
25–50 g (1–2 oz) cheese, grated
dab Marmite
1 teaspoon (5 ml) tomato purée
125 ml (5 fl oz) milk
1 egg, beaten
salt and pepper

Pre-heat the oven to 180°C/350°F/Gas 4. Pile cheese on to one slice of buttered bread and spread the other with Marmite and tomato purée. Sandwich together and cut into 4 triangles. Place in a small ovenproof dish. Beat together the milk and egg. Season. Pour over the sandwich, pushing the bread into the milk and egg mixture to ensure it gets well coated. Bake for 25–35 minutes until top is browned.

Cheese and tomato vegetables

Serves 1

This is a really useful recipe to master as it is very easy and cheap.

> 1 onion, chopped
> 2 cloves garlic, chopped
> 100 g (4 oz) mushrooms, sliced
> 1 small courgette, quartered and sliced
> 2 tablespoons (30 ml) oil
> 3 tomatoes, quartered and sliced
> 2 tablespoons (30 ml) tomato purée
> 25 g (1 oz) cheese, grated
> salt and pepper

Fry the onion, garlic, mushrooms and courgette in the oil for 10 minutes. Add the tomatoes and tomato purée and cook for a further 5 minutes. Stir in the cheese and season. Serve with pasta or as a topping for baked potatoes.

Cheese and potato cakes

Serves 1

> 200 g (8 oz) potatoes, cut into chunks
> 1 egg, beaten
> 50 g (2 oz) cheese, grated
> 2 spring onions, chopped
> salt and pepper
> dried wholemeal crumbs *or* wholemeal flour for coating
> oil for frying

Cook potatoes in boiling water until tender (about 15 minutes). Drain, mash and mix with egg, cheese and onions. Season. As soon as the mixture is cool enough to handle, divide into two portions and gently shape into two cakes. Coat with crumbs or flour and leave to stand for 30 minutes. Use enough oil to coat the bottom of a frying pan, heat and cook the cakes for 2 minutes on each side until brown.

Quick fried cheese 'n' tomato pizza
Serves 1–2

    150 g (6 oz) self-raising flour
    pinch salt
    1 tablespoon (15 ml) oil
    oil to grease frying pan
    2 tablespoons (30 ml) tomato purée
    sprinkling oregano
    1 tomato, sliced
    25 g (1 oz) cheese, grated

Pre-heat the grill. Mix the flour, salt and oil together with enough warm water (about 6 tablespoons (90 ml)) to make a dough. Knead for a couple of minutes until dough is pliable. Grease large frying pan lightly with oil. Press out dough to fill the pan. Fry for 4 minutes then turn dough and fry other side. Spread with the tomato purée, sprinkle the oregano over it, and top with the tomato slices and cheese. Grill until cheese melts and is bubbly.

Quick fried cheese 'n' mushroom pizza
Substitute 100 g (4 oz) mushrooms for the tomato. Gently fry mushrooms in some butter before starting to make the pizza, then cook as above.

Pasta and mushrooms with hummus sauce ☾

Serves 1

> 75 g (3 oz) pasta
> 1 small onion, chopped
> 1 clove garlic, chopped
> oil for frying
> 100 g (4 oz) mushrooms, sliced
> 100 g (4 oz) hummus
> 1 tablespoon (15 ml) milk
> salt and pepper

Add your chosen pasta to a saucepan of boiling water. While it's cooking (about 10–12 minutes) make the sauce. Fry the onion and garlic in oil until they start to colour. Add mushrooms and continue to cook until soft. Stir in the hummus and milk. Cover and simmer gently for a few minutes. When pasta is cooked, drain. Season the sauce and serve with the pasta.

Avocado and banana with pasta ❁☾

Serves 1

This is a particular favourite of mine. It is full of calories, but very easy to make and very tasty.

> 75 g (3 oz) pasta
> 1 tablespoon (15 ml) soft margarine
> 1 tablespoon (15 ml) smooth peanut butter
> 1 ripe avocado, peeled, stoned and chopped
> 1 ripe banana, chopped
> black pepper

Cook the pasta in boiling water until 'al dente' (cooked but still retaining some 'bite'). Beat together the margarine and peanut butter. When pasta is cooked, drain and add the other ingredients. Season with black pepper. Put back on the heat briefly to warm ingredients through. Serve immediately.

Tomato provençale and spaghetti

Serves 1

> 75 g (3 oz) spaghetti
> 200-g can tomatoes
> 2 mushrooms, sliced
> 1 clove garlic, crushed
> pinch mixed herbs
> 2 tablespoons (30 ml) oil

Cook the spaghetti in boiling water. Drain the tomatoes, reserving half of the juice and chop roughly. Fry the tomatoes, garlic and mushrooms in the oil. Add the reserved juice and herbs and simmer until spaghetti is ready. Then drain the spaghetti, pour the sauce over it and serve.

Mushnut sauce (for pasta)

Serves 1

> 1 onion, chopped
> 1 clove garlic, crushed
> 100 g (4 oz) mushrooms, sliced
> 2 tablespoons (30 ml) oil
> 1 teaspoon (5 ml) tomato purée
> 1 tablespoon (15 ml) roasted chopped hazelnuts
> 2 tablespoons (30 ml) crème fraîche
> salt and pepper

Fry onion, garlic and mushrooms in oil until soft. Add the tomato purée, hazelnuts and crème fraîche, plus 3 tablespoons (45 ml) water. Stir until it has heated through, season and serve with pasta.

Green lentil sauce (for pasta)
Serves 1

> 50 g (2 oz) green lentils
> 2 tablespoons (30 ml) creamy pesto

Cook the green lentils in boiling water for 10 minutes, then simmer for a further 20. Drain, mix in the pesto and serve with pasta.

Red lentil sauce (for pasta)
Serves 1

> 25 g (1 oz) split red lentils
> 1 teaspoon (5 ml) Marmite
> 1 tablespoon (15 ml) tomato ketchup

Boil the lentils in 250 ml (10 fl oz) water for 15 minutes, until cooked and reduced to a runny sauce. Add Marmite and ketchup, stir well and use to top pasta or a baked potato.

Vegetarian bolognese sauce
Makes 2 portions

Use half this recipe as a topping for spaghetti and keep half to use the next day in vegetarian bolognese bake (see page 28). It can also be used as a filling for baked potatoes.

1 onion, chopped
2 cloves garlic, crushed
1 large carrot, finely diced
1 tablespoon (15 ml) oil
100 g (4 oz) mushrooms, chopped
1 tablespoon (15 ml) tomato purée
250-g can chopped tomatoes
50 g (2 oz) bulghur wheat
1 tablespoon (15 ml) soy sauce

Fry the onion, garlic and carrot in the oil for 5 minutes. Add the mushrooms and continue to cook for 5 minutes. Add the remaining ingredients, pour in 200 ml (8 fl oz) water and bring to the boil. Cover and simmer for 15 minutes.

Carrot and courgette stir-fry
Serves 1

1 carrot, cut into matchsticks
1 courgette, cut into matchsticks
1 teaspoon (5 ml) oil
225-g can pineapple pieces, drained but reserve
    1 tablespoon (15 ml) pineapple juice
1 tablespoon (15 ml) tomato ketchup
1 tablespoon (15 ml) soy sauce
1 teaspoon (5 ml) wine vinegar
½ teaspoon (2.5 ml) cornflour

Stir-fry the carrot and courgette in the oil for 3–4 minutes. Add pineapple pieces. Mix together the other ingredients, add to the pan and simmer for 2–3 minutes until heated through.

Veggies in cheese sauce ◷

Serves 1

This is a useful recipe for a quick supper. Sometimes I add a little cream to the sauce and just serve it with crusty French bread.

150 g (6 oz) cauliflower florets
100 g (4 oz) carrots, sliced
50 g (2 oz) frozen peas
1 tablespoon (15 ml) margarine
1 tablespoon (15 ml) plain flour
1 teaspoon (5 ml) French mustard
125 ml (5 fl oz) milk
50 g (2 oz) cheese, grated

Cook the cauliflower and carrots in boiling water for 7 minutes. Add the peas and continue to cook for 3 minutes. Drain. Meanwhile make the sauce. Melt the margarine in a small pan, remove from the heat, stir in the flour and mustard, and gradually add just enough milk to make a smooth sauce. Return to the heat and as sauce thickens add the remaining milk. Cook for 1 minute, then add cheese. Mix with the cooked vegetables. Serve with rice or pasta.

Stir-fried vegetables with noodles ⏱

Serves 1–2

  85-g (3-oz) Doll instant noodles with wonton-flavoured
    soup base
  1 carrot, thinly sliced
  2 sticks celery, thinly sliced
  50 g (2 oz) mushrooms, thinly sliced
  1 tablespoon (15 ml) oil
  3 spring onions, thinly sliced
  ½ 190-g can sweetcorn
  ½ 350-g can beansprouts
  1 tablespoon (15 ml) soy sauce
  sprinkling peanuts or sesame seeds

Using 375 ml (15 fl oz) boiling water, cook noodles as directed on packet. Stir-fry the carrot, celery and mushrooms in the oil for 2 minutes. Add the spring onions, sweetcorn and beansprouts and continue stir-frying for another 2 minutes. Sieve the noodles and add to the pan. Cook for 2 minutes. Stir in soy sauce and peanuts or sesame seeds and serve.

10-minute curry
Serves 1

Well, I can cook this in 10 minutes! It depends on how quick you are at chopping up vegetables. Heat the oil while you prepare your veg, unless you are particularly slow – then you may risk burning the oil before you're ready to start.

    1 onion, chopped
    1 clove garlic, crushed
    100 g (4 oz) mushrooms, sliced
    1 tablespoon (15 ml) oil
    2 teaspoons (10 ml) balti paste
    1 teaspoon (5 ml) tomato purée
    200-g can curried baked beans
    1 tablespoon (15 ml) mango chutney (optional)
    1 tablespoon (15 ml) crème fraîche (optional)

Fry the onion, garlic and mushrooms in the oil for 5 minutes. Stir in the balti paste and the tomato purée and cook for 1 minute. Pour in 150 ml (6 fl oz) boiling water and simmer for 2 minutes. Add the beans, and the optional ingredients, if you're using them, and heat through. Serve.

Chick pea curry
Serves 1

You can use fresh chopped mint or mint sauce with this – but don't use dried mint.

    1 onion, chopped
    1 clove garlic, crushed
    1 tablespoon (15 ml) oil
    1 tablespoon (15 ml) balti paste
    200-g can chopped tomatoes
    400-g can chick peas, drained
    1 tablespoon (15 ml) mint, chopped *or* mint sauce

Fry onion and garlic in oil until soft. Stir in balti paste and cook for 1 minute. Add tomatoes and chick peas and simmer for 10 minutes. Add mint just before serving.

Fruity curry sauce ✿🕐
Serves 1

This is a very easy sauce, that you will probably use time and time again.

> 1 onion, diced
> 1 tablespoon (15 ml) oil
> 2 tablespoons (30 ml) balti paste
> 1 tablespoon (15 ml) tomato purée
> 1 tablespoon (15 ml) mango chutney
> 2 tablespoons (30 ml) crème fraîche
> 1–2 tablespoons (15–30 ml) chopped fresh coriander

Fry the onion in the oil until soft. Stir in the balti paste and tomato purée and cook for 2 minutes. Pour in 150 ml (6 fl oz) boiling water and simmer for 5 minutes. Now add the rest of the ingredients and the sauce is ready to serve mixed with cooked vegetables, beans or hard-boiled eggs.

Lentil and coconut dhal
Serves 1

> 2 tablespoons (30 ml) desiccated coconut
> 1 onion, chopped
> 1 clove garlic, crushed
> 2 tablespoons (30 ml) oil
> 2 teaspoons (10 ml) balti paste
> 50 g (2 oz) split red lentils
> knob of butter

Put the coconut into a bowl and just cover with boiling water. Leave to stand for 30 minutes. Fry the onion and garlic in the oil for 5 minutes. Add the balti paste and stir-fry for 2 minutes. Add the lentils and 150 ml (6 fl oz) boiling water and simmer for 20 minutes, adding more water if necessary. Finally, add the coconut and stir in a knob of butter. Serve immediately with rice.

Lentil and bulghur kedgeree
Serves 1

> 25 g (1 oz) green lentils
> 50 g (2 oz) bulghur wheat
> 1 onion, sliced
> 1 carrot, cut into matchsticks
> 1 teaspoon (5 ml) oil
> 2 teaspoons (10 ml) balti paste

Boil the green lentils in plenty of water for 10 minutes. Then reduce the heat and simmer for 10 minutes. Add the bulghur and continue to cook for 15 minutes. Meanwhile, fry the onion and carrot in the oil until they start to colour. Add the balti paste and cook for 1 minute, stirring. Pour in 100 ml (4 fl oz) boiling water, stir well and simmer for 5 minutes. When the lentils and bulghur are cooked, drain and mix with curried vegetables.

Cheese omelette ✿🕙
Serves 1

> 2–3 eggs, beaten
> 1 tablespoon (1   ml) milk *or* cold water
> 50 g (2 oz) cheese, grated
> salt and pepper
> knob of butter

Beat the eggs and milk or water. Add half the cheese and season. Melt the butter in a small frying pan. Pour in the egg mixture and swirl over the bottom of the pan. Draw the cooked egg into the middle, allowing the uncooked mixture to run underneath and set. When the egg has set, sprinkle the remaining cheese on top. Slide the omelette on to your plate, folding one half of the omelette over the other.

Mushroom omelette
Gently fry 100 g (4 oz) sliced button mushrooms in some butter until soft. Keep to one side while you cook the omelette as above but omitting the cheese. Add the mushrooms to the cooked omelette before sliding on to your plate.

Piperade
Serves 1

1 small onion, chopped
1 clove garlic, chopped
½ red pepper, diced
2 tablespoons (30 ml) oil
1 tomato, peeled and chopped
2 eggs, beaten
salt and pepper

Fry the onion, garlic and pepper in the oil until soft. Add the tomato and cook for 1 minute. Pour in the eggs and stir until the eggs are lightly scrambled. Season and serve.

Chinese rice with omelette
Serves 1

100 g (4 oz) basmati rice
250 ml (10 fl oz) vegetable stock
25 g (1 oz) butter
50 g (2 oz) mushrooms, sliced
1 tablespoon (15 ml) frozen peas
3 spring onions, chopped
1 egg, beaten
1 tablespoon (15 ml) milk
salt and pepper
1 tablespoon (15 ml) soy sauce

Put rice and stock in a saucepan and bring to the boil. Cover and simmer for 10–12 minutes until all the stock has been absorbed. Meanwhile, melt half the butter and stir-fry the mushrooms, peas and spring onions for 3–4 minutes. Set aside. Beat together the egg and milk and season. Melt the rest of the butter in a small frying pan and pour in the egg mixture. Tilt the pan so that the egg covers the bottom of the pan. Draw the cooked egg into the middle of the pan, allowing the uncooked mixture to run underneath and set. When the egg has set, slide on to a plate, roll it up and cut into little egg rolls. When rice is cooked add the soy sauce and mix in the stir-fried vegetables. Put in a bowl and serve with the egg rolls on top.

Broad bean, onion and coriander pilaff ☻

Serves 1

You really need fresh coriander for this dish. If you cannot get it, substitute fresh mint or mint sauce.

> 75 g (3 oz) basmati rice
> 2 onions, sliced
> 2 tablespoons (30 ml) oil
> 2 tablespoons (30 ml) fresh coriander, chopped
> 300-g can broad beans, drained

Cook the basmati rice in boiling water. Meanwhile, fry the onion in oil until quite brown. When the rice is cooked, mix in the coriander, the beans and half the fried onion. Arrange the remainder of the onions on top and serve.

Quick chilli 'n' tomato sauce ☻

Serves 1

> 1 tablespoon (15 ml) chilli relish
> 1 tablespoon (15 ml) tomato purée
> 1 tablespoon (15 ml) boiling water.

Mix all ingredients together and use as a sauce for savoury dishes.

3 Cooking with Friends

This is where the fun starts. We had some great laughs while busily preparing meals. It's when people come together at the end of the day that you get to hear all the latest gossip, find out what's going on in the world, and learn what's planned for the evening, weekend – and get the reports on what happened last night . . .

If you have nothing particular planned for an evening, why not invite a friend or two over for a meal? A leisurely meal followed by a trip to the bar was one of our favourite ways of spending the evening (winning hands down every time over *really* getting to grips with that essay).

If you are living in a communal household, although it is not usual to cook for everyone every night, it is common to have a kitty for some items, such as milk, bread, tea and coffee. (It is also common to have arguments about who's paid, who's finished the milk and so on!) If someone offers to cook one evening, the cost of the meal is divided between those taking part.

If you are living in a shared house, hopefully you will not have the problem of people nicking your foodstuffs (or at least they should be able to provide a plausible

excuse as to why they did so!) You should therefore be able to make more use of fresh vegetables in your cooking. You will soon find that an additional bonus is that it works out cheaper per head to cook in quantity.

Bulghur wheat salad with peanut sauce ☾

Serves 2–4

100 g (4 oz) bulghur wheat
knob of butter
100 g (4 oz) mushrooms, sliced
1 avocado, peeled, stoned and diced
3 tomatoes, skinned

Peanut sauce
150 g (6 oz) crunchy peanut butter
2 tablespoons (30 ml) soy sauce
1 tablespoon (15 ml) soft brown sugar
1 tablespoon (15 ml) lemon juice

Cook the bulghur wheat in boiling water for 10–15 minutes until tender; drain well. Melt the butter in a pan and cook mushrooms for 3–4 minutes; mix with other salad ingredients. Gently heat the peanut butter, soy sauce, sugar, lemon juice and 100 ml (4 fl oz) water and beat well to form a sauce. Pour over salad.

Curried bean and fruit salad ❂☾

Serves 4

1 onion, chopped
1 clove garlic, crushed
1 tablespoon (15 ml) oil
1 tablespoon (15 ml) curry paste
225-g can pineapple pieces in pineapple juice
1 banana, sliced
400-g can chick peas, drained
400-g can red kidney beans, drained

Fry the onion and garlic in the oil for 7 minutes until soft and starting to colour. Add the curry paste and the contents of the can of pineapple, including the juice. Simmer gently for 3 minutes. Add the remaining ingredients and stir well. Cool before serving.

Pasta salad

Serves 4–5

250 g (10 oz) pasta bows
1 onion, chopped
1 red pepper, diced
1 clove garlic, crushed
1 tablespoon (15 ml) oil
1 courgette, diced
100 g (4 oz) mushrooms, sliced

Dressing
1 clove garlic, crushed
1 teaspoon (5 ml) salt
½ teaspoon (2.5 ml) mustard powder
1 tablespoon (15 ml) lemon juice
2 tablespoons (30 ml) oil

Cook pasta in boiling water until 'al dente', then drain. Meanwhile fry onion, pepper and garlic in the oil for 5 minutes, add courgette and mushrooms and cook for a further 5 minutes. Add to pasta. Mix all dressing ingredients together, pour over the pasta and vegetables and stir well.

Rice salad

Serves 4

This is a great, really fresh tasting salad. Prepare it just before you are ready to eat as it tastes much better freshly dressed.

200 g (8 oz) brown rice, cooked and cooled
198-g can sweetcorn, drained
100 g (4 oz) frozen peas, cooked and cooled
2–3 tomatoes, skinned and chopped

Dressing
1 clove garlic, crushed
1 teaspoon (5 ml) salt
½ teaspoon (2.5 ml) mustard powder
1 tablespoon (15 ml) lemon juice
2 tablespoons (30 ml) low-fat natural yoghurt

Combine all the salad ingredients. Mix all the dressing ingredients. Pour dressing over salad, stir well and serve immediately.

Coleslaw with apple

Serves 3–4

200 g (8 oz) white cabbage, thinly sliced
100 g (4 oz) carrot, grated
100 g (4 oz) apple, grated
2 tablespoons (30 ml) mayonnaise
1 dessertspoon (10 ml) white wine vinegar
salt and pepper

Put the cabbage, carrot and apple in a bowl. Mix together the mayonnaise and vinegar and pour into the bowl. Stir thoroughly. Season.

Shortcrust pastry ✪ ⏱
Makes 12 oz (300 g)

Although you can buy pastry either frozen or chilled, here are some recipes that you may want to try. Don't worry if you have trouble rolling out your pastry – you can press it into your dish.

8 oz (200 g) flour
pinch of salt
5 oz (125 g) butter
cold water

Put the flour, salt and butter into a bowl. Rub the mixture between your fingertips until it resembles fine breadcrumbs. Add a few tablespoons of water – only as much as you need to form a dough. Wrap the dough in clingfilm and rest it in the fridge for 20 minutes before using. Roll out on a floured surface with a rolling pin, handling the dough as little as possible.

Cheese pastry
Add 3 oz (75 g) grated cheese, a pinch of dried mustard powder and an egg yolk to the 'breadcrumb' mixture.

Nutty pastry
Add 2 oz (50 g) roasted chopped hazelnuts and an egg yolk to the 'breadcrumb' mixture.

Baking 'blind'
This helps to produce a crispy pastry shell for quiches. Pre-heat the oven to 190°C/375°F/Gas 5. Line a 20-cm (8-in) flan tin with the pastry, then prick the base of the pastry all over with a fork. Put some greaseproof paper in the bottom and weigh down with some coins. Bake for 15 minutes. Remove paper and coins before using.

Broccoli, cheese and tomato quiche ✪
Serves 3–4

To skin tomatoes, put them in a bowl, cover with boiling water and leave until skin can be easily peeled away. Be careful when taking the tomatoes out as the water will still be very hot!

300 g (12 oz) cheese pastry (see page 48)
150 g (6 oz) broccoli florets, cooked
2 plum tomatoes, skinned and cut into wedges
75 g (3 oz) cheese, grated
2 eggs, beaten
125-ml carton single cream
salt and pepper
few chopped fresh herbs, such as chives (optional)

Pre-heat the oven to 190°C/375°F/Gas 5. Bake pastry blind (see page 48). Fill with broccoli, tomatoes and half the cheese. Mix together the eggs and cream, and season well, adding herbs if using. Pour into pastry case. Sprinkle with remaining cheese and bake for 35–45 minutes. Best served just warm or cold.

Mushroom quiche ✪
Serves 3–4

300 g (12 oz) nutty pastry (see page 48)
200 g (8 oz) mushrooms, sliced
small knob of butter
75 g (3 oz) cheese, grated
2 eggs, beaten
125-ml carton single cream
salt and pepper
few chopped fresh herbs, such as chives (optional)

Pre-heat the oven to 190°C/375°F/Gas 5. Bake pastry blind (see page 48). Fry mushrooms gently in butter for 1–2 minutes. Put in pastry case with half the cheese and herbs, if using. Beat together the eggs and cream, season and pour into pastry case. Sprinkle with remaining cheese and bake for 35–45 minutes. Best served just warm or cold.

Pizza dough
Enough to make 1 30-cm (12-in) pizza

> 200 g (8 oz) strong white bread flour
> 1 teaspoon (5 ml) salt
> 1 teaspoon (5 ml) sugar
> 1 teaspoon (5 ml) easy blend yeast
> 1 teaspoon (5 ml) oil

Mix all ingredients together, add 125 ml (5 fl oz) hand-hot water, then knead for 5 minutes. Leave the dough to rise in a covered bowl for 45 minutes. Before using, knead once more until smooth.

Quick pizza
Serves 4

> 400-g can chopped tomatoes
> 1 tablespoon (15 ml) tomato purée
> sprinkling oregano
> 2 large pizza bases
> 6 mini cheeses from the pick 'n' mix section,
>   *or* 100–150 g (4–6 oz) cheese
> 2 tablespoons (30 ml) sweetcorn
> 2 tablespoons (30 ml) pineapple pieces
> black pepper

Pre-heat the oven to 230°C/450°F/Gas 8. Simmer the tomatoes, tomato purée and oregano for 10–15 minutes until you have a thick sauce. Divide this between the pizza bases, coating them evenly. Slice the cheese over the tomato mixture, then top with the sweetcorn and pineapple. Bake for 12–15 minutes.

Pizza casa
Serves 2–4

We visited Italy this year. (The last time I had been there was on
a Eurorail ticket – which I no longer qualify for.) We stayed in
beautiful Ravello, where I was overcome by the quality of the
fresh produce. This simple pizza was inspired by our stay
there.

> 1 quantity pizza dough (see page 50)
> 1 quantity tomato sauce (see below)
> few basil leaves, shredded
> 4 sun-dried tomatoes, sliced
> 75 g (3 oz) mozzarella, grated
> salt and pepper

Pre-heat the oven to 200°C/400°F/Gas 6. Roll the dough out
into a 30-cm (12-in) circle. Place on a large baking sheet and
prick all over with a fork. Spread with tomato sauce. Arrange
basil leaves and sun-dried tomatoes on top and sprinkle with
cheese. Bake for 25–35 minutes.

Tomato sauce (for pizza)
Makes enough to cover 1 30-cm (12-in) pizza

> 1 garlic clove, crushed
> 1 tablespoon (15 ml) oil
> 400-g can chopped tomatoes
> 1 tablespoon (15 ml) tomato purée

Gently fry the garlic in the oil for 1 minute. Add the remaining
ingredients and simmer gently until you have a thick sauce
(approximately 20 minutes). It should be thick enough so that,
when a spoon is pushed through it, you can see the bottom of
the pan and the sauce remains separated.

Tomato and aubergine sauce (for pasta)   ✪
Serves 4

 1 onion, chopped
 2 cloves garlic, crushed
 3 tablespoons (45 ml) oil
 1 aubergine, diced
 400-g can chopped tomatoes
 1 tablespoon (15 ml) tomato purée
 sprinkling oregano
 salt and pepper

Fry the onion and garlic in 1 tablespoon (15 ml) oil for 5 minutes, add the aubergine and the remaining oil and continue to cook until soft (5–10 minutes). Add the rest of the ingredients and seasoning and simmer gently for 30 minutes. Serve with pasta.

Creamy lentil sauce (for pasta)   ◔
Serves 4

 150 g (6 oz) split red lentils
 1 teaspoon (5 ml) Marmite
 2 onions, finely chopped
 2 cloves garlic, crushed
 200 g (8 oz) mushrooms, chopped
 2 tablespoons (30 ml) oil
 125 g (5 oz) lite cream cheese, garlic and herb flavour
 2 tablespoons (30 ml) fresh parsley, chopped

Put the lentils and Marmite in a small sauce pan and cover with boiling water. Boil for 10 minutes, topping up with boiling water as necessary. Fry the onions, garlic and mushrooms in the oil until nicely golden. When the lentils have been reduced to a medium-thick purée, add the vegetables, cream cheese and parsley. Stir to heat through and serve with pasta.

Chick peas with banana and mango ◐◕
Serves 4

This is a dish I'm surprised I haven't thought of before – it's just so incredibly quick and easy to make and utterly delicious.

2 x 430-g can chick peas, drained
4 bananas, thickly sliced
340-g jar of hot and spicy mango chutney
300 g natural Greek-style yoghurt

Place all the ingredients in a saucepan and heat gently. Do not boil. When heated through thoroughly, serve with rice.

Aubergine, mushroom and coriander balti ◐◕
Serves 2

Balti paste has made it much easier to prepare home-made curries in only a few minutes. This is currently one of our favourite recipes.

1 aubergine, diced
4 tablespoons (60 ml) oil
100 g (4 oz) mushrooms, sliced
1 onion, sliced
1 clove garlic, crushed
5 tablespoons (75 g) balti paste
2 tablespoons chopped fresh coriander

Fry the aubergine in the oil for 5–6 minutes, then add the mushrooms, onion and garlic, and continue cooking for a further 5 minutes. Stir in the balti paste and stir-fry for 5 minutes. Finally, mix in the coriander and serve.

Veggie bolognese and polenta ☺

Serves 2

120-g packet Beanfeast, bolognese style
400-g can chopped tomatoes
225 g instant polenta
1 teaspoon (5 ml) salt

Put the Beanfeast, tomatoes and 500 ml (1 pint) water into a large saucepan. Bring to the boil and then simmer gently for 15 minutes. Bring 750 ml (1½ pints) water to the boil and add the polenta and salt. Stir with a wooden spoon while cooking for 5–10 minutes. Serve with the bolognese beans.

Ratatouille ✪

Serves 4

1 onion, chopped
2 cloves garlic, chopped
1 red pepper, chopped
2 tablespoons (30 ml) oil
2 courgettes, chopped
1 aubergine, chopped
400-g can chopped tomatoes with basil
black pepper

Fry the onion, garlic and pepper in the oil for 10 minutes. Add the courgettes and aubergine and cook for a further 10 minutes. Pour in the tomatoes and season with black pepper. Cover and simmer gently for 40 minutes. Can be served hot or cold.

Oven-baked ratatouille ⊛
Serves 4

I think ratatouille is best served just warm but it can also be served cold as a salad. I have found that this makes a great filling for lasagne as well (see page 57).

> 200 g (8 oz) courgette, sliced
> 200 g (8 oz) aubergine, diced
> 1 orange pepper, diced
> 1 yellow pepper, diced
> 1 red onion, sliced
> 4 tomatoes, cut into wedges
> 4 tablespoons (60 ml) oil
> salt and pepper

Pre-heat oven to 220°C/425°F/Gas 7. Mix everything together, making sure that the vegetables are well coated with oil. Spread over a roasting or baking tray and bake for 40 minutes until the vegetables are starting to crisp at the edges. Serve warm or cold with rice or pasta.

Macaroni cheese
Serves 4

A childhood recipe that people either love or hate. I have added some vegetables to make it an all-in-one dish. On a cold winter night, however, it is lovely with some crisp wholemeal rolls. Although I have given a recipe for cheese sauce, you will also find some very good tubs of fresh cheese sauce in the chilled cabinets of large supermarkets.

> 200 g (8 oz) broccoli
> 1 cauliflower (approximately 200 g/(8 oz)
> 200 g (8 oz) quick cook macaroni
> 400 ml (16 fl oz) cheese sauce (see page 87)
> 2 teaspoons (10 ml) French mustard
> black pepper
> knob of butter (for greasing)
> 75 g (3 oz) fresh breadcrumbs
> 100 g (4 oz) cheese, grated

Pre-heat the oven to 180°C/350°F/Gas 4. Divide the broccoli and cauliflower into florets and boil until just tender, but still with a little 'bite' – about 5 minutes. Meanwhile, cook the macaroni in boiling water until tender – about 4 minutes. Mix together the cooked vegetables and macaroni with the cheese sauce, mustard and black pepper. Pour into a greased oven-proof dish and cover with the breadcrumbs and cheese. Bake for 30 minutes or until the top is brown and crisp.

Macaroni cheese with tomatoes
To the cooked vegetables add a 200-g can chopped tomatoes or a few fresh tomatoes, skinned and sliced roughly. (To skin tomatoes, put in a small bowl and pour boiling water over them. After a couple of minutes, the skin can be easily removed. When taking the tomatoes out, use a fork as the water will still be hot!) Then mix 2 tablespoons (30 ml) tomato purée with 2 tablespoons (30 ml) oil and spread over the mixed vegetables, macaroni and cheese sauce, *before* you add the breadcrumbs and cheese. Yummy! Heat freaks can also add chilli powder or sauce to taste to the tomato purée mix.

Cheese and mushroom cannelloni
Serves 4

2 onions, diced
200 g (8 oz) mushrooms, diced
2 cloves garlic, crushed
2 tablespoons (30 ml) oil
250-g tub ricotta cheese
100 g (4 oz) cheese, grated
12 cannelloni pasta tubes
400 ml (16 fl oz) cheese sauce (see page 87)
2 tablespoons (30 ml) tomato purée
sprinkling oregano
1 tablespoon (15 ml) oil
1 tablespoon (15 ml) chilli sauce (optional)

Pre-heat the oven to 200°C/400°F/Gas 6. Cook the onions, mushrooms and garlic in the oil for 10 minutes. Stir in the ricotta and half the grated cheese. Use this mixture to stuff the cannelloni tubes. Pour half the cheese sauce into a greased lasagne dish and arrange the tubes on top. Mix together the tomato purée, oregano, 2 tablespoons (30 ml) water, oil and chilli sauce, if using, and spread over the rolls. Spoon the rest of the cheese sauce on top and sprinkle with remaining cheese. Bake for 35 minutes until brown on top.

Ratatouille filled lasagne rolls
Serves 4–6

12 sheets fresh lasagne
oven-baked ratatouille (see page 55)
500 ml (1 pint) cheese sauce (see page 87)
75 g (3 oz) cheese, grated

Pre-heat the oven to 180°C/350°F/Gas 4. Soak the lasagne in boiling water for 5 minutes, drain. Lay out the pasta and divide the ratatouille between the sheets, spreading evenly over them. Roll pasta up around the ratatouille and place rolls in a lasagne dish. Cover with cheese sauce and sprinkle with cheese. Bake for 30 minutes.

Undercover beans
Serves 4

This is delicious! Tortilla chips make a great topping for casse-roles and we are using them more and more. It doesn't matter what size packet you get, you can use the rest for nibbles before dinner.

  1 onion, chopped
  2 cloves garlic, crushed
  100 g (4 oz) mushrooms, sliced
  3 tablespoons (45 ml) oil
  200 g (8 oz) aubergine, diced
  400-g can chopped tomatoes
  2 x 440-g can beans in chilli sauce
  packet tortilla chips
  150-ml carton sour cream
  75 g (3 oz) cheese, grated

Pre-heat the oven to 180°C/350°F/Gas 4. Fry the onion, garlic and mushrooms in the oil for 2–3 minutes. Add the aubergine and continue to fry for 5 minutes. Transfer to a casserole dish and add the tomatoes and beans in chilli sauce. Cover and cook in the oven for 45 minutes. Remove from the oven. Spread a layer of tortilla chips over the surface of the mixture, pour the cream on top and sprinkle wit' the cheese. Return the casserole dish to the oven and continue cooking, uncovered, for 15 minutes.

Cheese 'n' lentil bake
Serves 3–4

200 g (8 oz) split red lentils
375 ml (15 fl oz) vegetable stock *or* boiling water with 1
    teaspoon (5 ml) Marmite
1 onion, diced
knob of butter
100 g (4 oz) cheese, grated
salt and pepper

Pre-heat the oven to 190°C/375°F/Gas 5. Cook the lentils in the stock or boiling water until tender (15–20 minutes), adding more water if needed. You want to end up with a thick purée. Meanwhile, cook the onion in the butter until it starts to colour. When the lentils are cooked, mash with the grated cheese and onion. Season. Place in a greased, lined 1-kg (2-lb) loaf tin. Cook in the oven for 50–60 minutes. Allow to cool in the tin for 5–10 minutes and then serve.

Lentil and courgette bake
Add 1 large grated courgette to the lentil mixture before baking.

Tomato and cheese topped bake
Instead of cooking the mixture in a loaf tin, put in a lasagne or casserole dish and top with slices of tomato and more grated cheese. Bake for 40–50 minutes.

Parsley and lentil bake
Add 1 tablespoon (15 ml) crème fraîche, a squeeze of lemon juice and 1 tablespoon (15 ml) chopped fresh parsley to the lentil mixture before baking.

Vegetable and bread bake
Serves 4

You should be able to buy ready prepared bags of mixed vegetables for stews. If you cannot find these, then make your own mix from carrots, turnips, parsnips and swedes.

1 onion, chopped
1 kg (2 lb) mixed stew vegetables, chopped
2 tablespoons (30 ml) oil
1 teaspoon (5 ml) oregano
1 teaspoon (5 ml) thyme
295-g can condensed cream of onion soup
400-g can cannelini beans
black pepper
3–4 slices bread, well buttered
1 teaspoon (5 ml) French mustard

Pre-heat the oven to 200°C/400°F/Gas 6. Fry the onion and stew vegetables in the oil for 5 minutes. Remove from heat, add the oregano, thyme and 125 ml (5 fl oz) boiling water, return to the boil and simmer for 10 minutes. Now mix in the soup and beans, season with black pepper. Pour into a casserole dish and cover with the sliced bread, buttered side up. Dot with the mustard and bake for 30 minutes.

Mexican chilli casserole
Serves 4

I found Vegemince in the freezer of a large supermarket; if you cannot find it use some diced vegetables or a dried variety of soya mince.

> 1 onion, chopped
> 1 red pepper, diced
> 1 green pepper, diced
> 2 tablespoons (30 ml) oil
> 450 g Vegemince
> 400-g can chopped tomatoes
> 400-g can beans in chilli sauce
> 150-ml carton sour cream
> tortilla chips
> 125 g (5 oz) mozzarella cheese, grated

Pre-heat the oven to 180°C/350°F/Gas 4. Fry the onion and peppers in oil for 5 minutes. Add Vegemince and stir to brown. Stir in the tomatoes and beans and pour into a large casserole dish. Cover and cook in the oven for 1 hour. Remove from oven and top with sour cream. Cover the surface with tortilla chips, then sprinkle with the cheese. Return to the oven and cook, uncovered, for 15 minutes.

Soya and apple casserole ⊛
Serves 3–4

Always on the lookout for new products to try, I found these dried soya chunks in Sainsbury's. Although soya is in itself rather bland it does take on other flavours well. This is one of two recipes that I made with a pack.

    75 g (3 oz) dried soya chunks
    1 onion, chopped
    1 green pepper, diced
    2 tablespoons (30 ml) oil
    100 g (4 oz) mushrooms, sliced
    400 g (1 lb) cooking apples, cored, peeled and cut into
        thick slices
    2 tablespoons (30 ml) tomato purée
    pinch sage
    375 ml (15 fl oz) dry cider *or* apple juice
    salt and pepper
    4 tablespoons (60 ml) cream (optional)

Rehydrate soya in boiling water for 10 minutes. Meanwhile fry onion and pepper in oil for 7 minutes, add mushrooms and apple and stir-fry for 3 minutes. Drain the soya and add to the mixture, with the tomato purée, sage and cider or apple juice. Season. Bring to the boil, cover and simmer for 20 minutes. Stir in cream, if using, and serve.

Soya and bean goulash ✿
Serves 3–4

    75 g (3 oz) dried soya chunks
    2 onions, chopped
    2 cloves garlic, crushed
    1 red pepper, diced
    1 green pepper, diced
    2 tablespoons (30 ml) oil
    400-g can chopped tomatoes
    400-g can red kidney beans in chilli sauce
    extra chilli powder *or* sauce (optional)
    natural yoghurt (to serve)

Pour boiling water over soya chunks and leave for 10 minutes. Fry onion, garlic and peppers in oil for 10 minutes. Drain the soya and add to the mixture, together with the tomatoes and kidney beans. Bring to the boil, cover and simmer for 20 minutes. Add extra chilli if required. Serve topped with yoghurt.

Beer fondue

Serves 2

My brother introduced me to this version and it is now just as popular as our original wine-based fondue. I like to use Ruddles beer, but I'm sure whichever your favourite beer is, will do! It's a strange thing that, considering how popular fondue sets used to be (almost *de rigueur* on wedding lists), I don't know many people who actually cook fondues. If you're lucky you may be able to borrow one from your parents' cupboard – after all if they never use it, why not let you have it?

> 250 ml (10 fl oz) beer
> 250 g (10 oz) cheese, grated
> 1 clove garlic, crushed
> 1 tablespoon (15 ml) cornflour, mixed with a little cold water
> 25 g (1 oz) butter
> 1 teaspoon (5 ml) French mustard
> French bread (for serving)

Place the beer, cheese and garlic in a saucepan. Heat gently until the cheese melts. Add the cornflour mixture, butter and mustard. Keep stirring until fondue thickens and bubbles. Serve in bowls with French bread to dip into the fondue.

4 The Blow-out Sunday Lunch

This is often the occasion that brings people to cook together for the first time. It needs some organisation. You must decide how many you are cooking for, what the menu is going to be, make out your shopping list, do the shopping, the cooking and, last but not least, the washing up! Once it is decided who will do what, this is much easier to organise than it sounds. Another option is that each person is totally responsible for one dish. But if you are doing it this way, you still need to make sure that everyone knows how much they have spent, so that you can add up the expenses and divide the total among you, to ensure that the person doing the main dish doesn't bear the brunt of the cost. I know some people prefer this second method but it can run into more problems . . . If someone doesn't get up in time, for instance, you may find yourself without some of your lunch!

Still, it is one of the pleasures of life to be able to sit down with some friends and a bottle or two and really pig out. The afternoon should be kept free as the stupor produced by these meals usually entails a siesta!

I remember one afternoon when some of us had booked a court to play badminton . . . What a waste of money! When the time came, nobody wanted to go and we couldn't bring ourselves to run about the court. We all stood about moaning 'yours' as the shuttlecock passed us by. A big mistake!

```
Menu 1

Nut roast
Tomato sauce
Grilled cheesy mash
French peas
Lemon and banana meringue pie
Drink: red wine
```

Cooking hints

It is easiest to cook the pie first and serve it cold. If you want to serve it hot, don't forget to turn up the temperature of the oven when you take out the nut roast.

Nut roast
Serves 6–8

This nut roast serves 6–8 so you will have enough for second helpings or to serve some cold the next day.

600 g (1½ lbs) parsnips, chopped
1 onion, chopped
2 celery sticks, chopped
1 clove garlic, crushed
100 g (4 oz) mushrooms, chopped
2 tablespoons (30 ml) oil
25 g (1 oz) butter
1 tablespoon (15 ml) fresh parsley
pinch dried thyme
salt and pepper
150 g (6 oz) peanuts, chopped
50 g (2 oz) roasted hazelnuts
100 g (4 oz) fresh breadcrumbs
1 egg, beaten

Pre-heat the oven to 200°C/400°F/Gas 6. Cook the parsnips in boiling water until tender. While they are cooking, fry the onion, celery, garlic and mushrooms in the oil until soft. When parsnips are cooked, drain and mash with the butter. Mix all ingredients together. Pour into a greased 1-kg (2-lb) loaf tin. Cover with foil and cook for 1–1¼ hours until roast is firm to the touch. Leave to stand in tin for 10 minutes before serving.

Tomato sauce (for nut roasts)
Serves 3–4

If you are serving nut roast just warm or cold then the best accompaniment is a tasty tomato sauce. This is our favourite – and can of course be used with other dishes as well. Passata can be found alongside tomato purée in supermarkets.

    1 onion, chopped
    2 tablespoons (30 ml) oil
    400-g can *or* packet of passata
    1 teaspoon (5 ml) sugar
    2 tablespoons (30 ml) wine vinegar

Fry the onion in 1 tablespoon (15 ml) of the oil for 5 minutes until soft. Add the remaining ingredients and simmer for 5 minutes.

Grilled cheesy mash
Serves 3–4

    800 g (2 lb) large potatoes, peeled and cut into large
       cubes
    knob of butter
    2 tablespoons (30 ml) milk
    1 teaspoon (5 ml) mustard powder
    100 g (4 oz) cheese, grated
    salt and pepper

Cook the potatoes in boiling water until soft – about 20 minutes. Drain well. Pre-heat the grill. Mash the potatoes with the butter, milk, mustard powder and half the cheese. Season well. Put into a shallow, heat-proof dish and sprinkle with the rest of the cheese. Grill until cheese melts and starts to bubble and brown. Serve immediately.

French peas
Serves 3–4

400 g (1 lb) frozen peas
1 dessertspoon (10 ml) sugar
few leaves from a little gem lettuce, shredded
2–3 spring onions, finely chopped
melted butter (to serve)

Cook the peas, adding the sugar to the water. When cooked, add the lettuce and onions and leave for 1 minute. Drain and serve with butter.

Lemon and banana meringue pie
Serves 4

This recipe came about because I had a banana which needed using up. I don't know why I hadn't thought of this combination before – it is utterly wonderful.

3 tablespoons (45 ml) cornflour
grated rind and juice of 2 lemons
175 g (7 oz) caster sugar
2 eggs, separated
1 sweet pastry shell
1 banana, sliced

Pre-heat the oven to 220°C/425°F/Gas 7. Blend the cornflour with 125 ml (5 fl oz) water and put in a small saucepan with the grated rind and juice of the lemons. Bring to the boil, stirring. Reduce the heat and add 100 g (4 oz) of the sugar, stirring until the sugar has dissolved. Remove from the heat and cool slightly. Beat the egg yolks and add them to the lemon mixture. Arrange the banana in the bottom of the pastry shell and spoon the lemon mixture over before levelling the top. Whisk the egg whites with half the remaining sugar. When stiff, fold in the remaining sugar and pile on to the lemon mixture, completely covering the lemon base. Bake for 10–15 minutes until meringue is crisp and slightly browned.

Menu 2

Vegetable and bean gratin
Baked basmati rice
Leaf salad
Rhubarb charlotte
Drink: wine or cider

Cooking hints

Turn up the temperature of the oven when the main course is served and put in pud 30 minutes before you wish to eat it.

Vegetable and bean gratin
Serves 4

2 aubergines, sliced
3 tablespoons (45 ml) oil
1 onion, chopped
2 cloves garlic, chopped
400-g can chopped tomatoes
1 tablespoon (15 ml) tomato purée
100 g (4 oz) chestnut mushrooms, thinly sliced
195-g jar Pastasciutta with artichokes
400-g can flageolet beans
75 g (3 oz) fresh wholemeal breadcrumbs
50 g (2 oz) Parmesan cheese

Pre-heat the grill. Put the aubergine slices on the grill and brush with some of the oil. Cook until brown. Turn, brush with oil and grill the other side. Pre-heat the oven to 180°C/350°F/ Gas 4. Fry the onion and garlic in remaining oil for about 10 minutes, until soft and golden. Add the tomatoes and tomato purée and continue to cook until you have a thick sauce. Pour half the sauce into an ovenproof dish. Cover with half the aubergine slices. Add the mushrooms, artichokes and beans. Top with the rest of the tomato sauce and aubergine slices. Mix together the breadcrumbs and Parmesan and use to cover the vegetables. Bake for 60 minutes.

Baked basmati rice
Serves 4–6

400 g (1 lb) basmati rice
600 ml (24 fl oz) vegetable stock

Pre-heat the oven to 180°C/350°F/Gas 4. Put the rice in a shallow casserole dish and pour in the stock. Cover dish with foil and cook for 35–45 minutes. (Cooking time will depend on the shape of your dish and how tightly it is covered.) Fluff rice up with a fork before serving.

Leaf salad
Serves 4–6

> 2 little gem lettuces, shredded
> ¼ iceberg lettuce, sliced
> 1 avocado, peeled, stoned and cubed
> 8 radishes, thinly sliced
> ½ cucumber, diced
>
> *Dressing*
> 6 tablespoons (90 ml) oil
> 2 tablespoons (30 ml) orange juice
> 1 tablespoon (15 ml) red wine vinegar
> pinch salt
> 1 teaspoon (5 ml) wholegrain mustard

Arrange salad ingredients in a serving bowl. Put all the dressing ingredients into a bottle or jar, shake vigorously and pour over salad just before serving.

Rhubarb charlotte
Serves 4

> 450 g (1 lb) rhubarb, cleaned and cubed
> 75 g (3 oz) butter
> 150 g (6 oz) fresh wholemeal breadcrumbs
> 1 teaspoon (5 ml) mixed spices
> 50 g (2 oz) brown sugar
> 2 tablespoons (30 ml) orange juice
> 2 tablespoons (30 ml) runny honey
> cream *or* custard (to serve)

Pre-heat the oven to 200°C/400°F/Gas 6. Fry the rhubarb in half the butter until soft. Remove from the pan. Fry the bread-crumbs in remaining butter until butter is absorbed and crumbs are browning. Layer the rhubarb and breadcrumbs in an ovenproof dish, finishing with a layer of crumbs. Mix the rest of the ingredients together and spoon over dish. Bake for 20 minutes and serve with cream or custard. Scrumptious!

Menu 3

Summer vegetable bake
Roasted new potatoes with rosemary
Carrots with lemon and ginger
Brioche and marmalade pudding
Drink: white wine

Cooking hints

Put the pud in when you take the main course out of the oven.

Summer vegetable bake
Serves 4

    25 g (1 oz) butter
    1 clove garlic, crushed
    1 aubergine, sliced
    2 onions, finely chopped
    1 yellow pepper, sliced
    1 tablespoon (15 ml) oil
    400-g can chopped tomatoes
    2 courgettes, halved and sliced
    250 g (10 oz) mushrooms, sliced
    1 tablespoon (15 ml) Parmesan cheese

Pre-heat the grill. Melt the butter, mix with the garlic and use to
coat the aubergine slices. Grill 4–5 minutes on each side until
nicely brown. Pre-heat the oven to 180°C/350°F/Gas 4. Cook
the onions and pepper in the oil for 10 minutes until brown.
Put half the tomatoes into an ovenproof dish. Add the courgettes, mushrooms and cooked onions and pepper. Cover with
the aubergine slices, and then top with the remaining tomatoes
and sprinkle with the Parmesan. Bake for 45 minutes.

Roasted new potatoes with rosemary
Serves 4

    450 g (1 lb) new potatoes, unpeeled
    2 tablespoons (30 ml) oil
    1 tablespoon (15 ml) rosemary, chopped
    1 clove garlic, crushed

Pre-heat the oven to 180°C/350°F/Gas 4. Cook the potatoes for
5 minutes in boiling water, drain and put into a bowl. Pour in
the oil, add the rosemary and garlic and stir to make sure the
potatoes are well covered with the mixture. Place on a roasting
tray and cook for 30 minutes until browned.

Carrots with lemon and ginger
Serves 4

>   400 g (1 lb) carrots, in small chunks
>   2 teaspoons (10 ml) ginger purée
>   juice of 1 lemon
>   25 g (1 oz) butter

Cook carrots in boiling water for 10–15 minutes until tender. Drain, add the remaining ingredients to the pan and cook until butter is absorbed and the carrots are starting to brown.

Brioche and marmalade pudding
Serves 4–6

You can of course make this with bread instead of brioche – but since we tried it with brioche we have never gone back to using bread.

>   4 brioche rolls
>   75–100 g (3–4 oz) butter, softened
>   3 tablespoons (45 ml) marmalade
>   400 ml (1 pint) milk
>   3 eggs, beaten

Pre-heat the oven to 180°C/350°F/Gas 4. Slice the brioche rolls and butter them. Place half the slices in an ovenproof dish and cover with the marmalade. Then top with the remaining brioche slices, buttered side up. Beat together the milk and eggs and pour over the brioche, pushing the slices down into the milk mixture. Bake for about 30–40 minutes until well risen and brown.

```
┌─────────────────────────────────────┐
│ Menu 4                              │
│                                     │
│ Aubergine dupiaza                   │
│ Bombay potatoes                     │
│ Cauliflower in nut cream sauce      │
│ Chillied peas                       │
│ Cucumber raita                      │
│ Indian bread                        │
│ Ice-cream or sorbet                 │
│ Drink: lager                        │
└─────────────────────────────────────┘
```

Cooking hints

If you are cooking all this on your own I suggest you put your oven on to 150°C/300°F/Gas 2, so that you can keep some dishes warm while you are cooking others. Start by preparing the cucumber raita. Then go on to the cauliflower and potato dishes. Prepare the coconut, onion and cauliflower, then pre-cook the potatoes. Now do the chillied peas and aubergine dupiaza (do not add the third onion and coriander to the aubergine yet). Put the chillied peas and aubergine dupiaza into the oven while cooking the Bombay potatoes and cauliflower in nut cream sauce. Finish off the aubergine. The Indian bread may need heating in the oven or grilling; check the pack/s. Choose a simple ice-cream or sorbet. You will want something refreshing, not rich, at the end of the meal. I suggest vanilla or coconut ice-cream, or lemon or passion fruit sorbet.

Aubergine dupiaza
Serves 4

> 1 aubergine, sliced
> 4 tablespoons (60 ml) oil
> 3 large onions
> 2 cloves garlic, crushed
> 1 teaspoon (5 ml) ginger purée
> 2 tablespoons (30 ml) balti paste
> 250 g natural yoghurt
> knob of butter
> 1 teaspoon (5 ml) brown sugar
> sprinkling coriander

Pre-heat the grill. Put the aubergine slices on the grill, brush with some of the oil and grill until brown. Turn and repeat. Chop 2 onions and cook with garlic and ginger in remaining oil for 10 minutes. Add balti paste and stir-fry for 2 minutes. Add aubergine and yoghurt and stir to heat through. Slice the third onion. Melt the butter in a small frying pan, add the sugar and fry the onion until very brown.

Pour the aubergine mixture into a bowl, pile the fried onion on top, sprinkle with coriander and serve.

Bombay potatoes
Serves 4

> 200 g (8 oz) new potatoes, halved
> 1 tablespoon (15 ml) Bombay spices
> 6 tablespoons (90 ml) oil

Boil the potatoes for 5 minutes, drain and pat dry. Fry the spices in the oil for 1 minute, and then add the potatoes. Stir-fry for a few minutes until brown.

Cauliflower in nut cream sauce
Serves 4

  4 tablespoons (60 ml) desiccated coconut
  1 cauliflower, divided into florets
  1 onion, chopped
  2 cloves garlic, crushed
  2 tablespoons (30 ml) oil
  2 tablespoons (30 ml) balti paste
  50 g (2 oz) ground almonds
  125-ml carton double cream

Put the coconut in a small bowl, just cover with boiling water and leave to stand for 30 minutes. Cook the cauliflower in boiling water for 5 minutes, then drain. Fry the onion and garlic in the oil for 5 minutes. Add the balti paste and stir-fry for 2 minutes. Add the cooked cauliflower and remaining ingredients and stir to heat through.

Chillied peas
Serves 2–4

  1 onion, chopped
  1 clove garlic, crushed
  1 tablespoon (15 ml) oil
  2 teaspoons (10 ml) balti paste
  chilli powder or sauce to taste
  100 g (4 oz) frozen peas
  200-g can chopped tomatoes

Fry the onion and garlic in oil for 5 minutes. Add the balti paste, chilli and peas and stir-fry for 2 minutes. Pour in the tomatoes. Bring to the boil, then cover and simmer for 10 minutes.

If serving this as the only vegetable, this quantity would really only stretch to two people.

Cucumber raita
Serves 4

> ¼ cucumber, finely diced
> 2 spring onions, sliced
> 2 tablespoons (30 ml) chopped fresh mint
> 250 g natural yoghurt

Mix all ingredients together and serve.

5 Classic Vegetarian Student Dishes

These are favourite dishes with students everywhere. Looking at them I think that one of the reasons for their popularity is that they are easy to make in quantity, and therefore great for entertaining. The other thing that strikes me is that, like a lot of student food, they are strongly flavoured. With their continuing popularity, these are good dishes to master as they will greatly improve your reputation as a cook!

Although I refer to these as 'classic', the recipes themselves are my current versions of the dishes. My cooking continues to change as I search for the 'perfect' recipes!

All these recipes can be altered to cater for different numbers. Just remember that if you require double the quantity it is often best to make the recipe twice rather than try to fit it into one large dish. Large quantities can take a lot longer to cook.

You can stretch your main dish to serve more people by serving salads, baked potatoes and garlic bread with it.

Spag no-bol
Serves 2   ⏴

A perennial favourite when entertaining a friend: what can be
nicer than a bowl of spaghetti and a glass of wine? We love
garlic bread with this dish (although a salad would be a
healthier alternative). Why not compromise and serve a salad
and garlic bread!

> 50 g (2 oz) split red lentils
> 1 onion, sliced
> 1 clove garlic, crushed
> 100 g (4 oz) mushrooms, chopped
> 2 tablespoons (30 ml) oil
> 200-g can chopped tomatoes
> 1 tablespoon (15 ml) tomato purée
> sprinkling oregano
> 150 g (6 oz) spaghetti

Cook the lentils in boiling water for 10 minutes. Fry the onion,
garlic and mushrooms in the oil for 10 minutes until soft. Add
to the lentils with the tomatoes, tomato purée and oregano.
Simmer gently for 5–10 minutes. Meanwhile, cook the spaghetti in boiling water and when ready, drain and serve with
the lentil mixture.

Garlic bread
Serves 4–6

> 1 French loaf
> 100 g (4 oz) butter, softened
> mixed herbs
> 2 cloves garlic, crushed
> poppy seeds (optional)

Pre-heat the oven to 200°C/400°F/Gas 6. Slice the loaf at about
2.5 cm (1 in) intervals to within 1 cm (½ in) of the base. Mix
together the butter, herbs and garlic and use to spread into the
cuts. Smear a little butter over the top of the loaf and sprinkle
with poppy seeds, if using. Wrap in foil and cook for 20–30
minutes. Serve hot.

Creamy vegetable and nut curry
Serves 4

This has to be one of the best curries that I have ever made. Please try it as it is easy to make and very, very good.

4 tablespoons (60 ml) desiccated coconut
1 aubergine (200 g/8 oz), diced
1 potato (200 g/8 oz), cut into matchsticks
200 g (8 oz) carrot, diced
100 g (4 oz) frozen peas
1 onion, sliced
2 cloves garlic, crushed
3 tablespoons (45 ml) oil
2 tablespoons (30 ml) balti paste
1 tablespoon (15 ml) tomato purée
4 tablespoons (60 ml) ground almonds
125-ml carton double cream

Put the coconut into a bowl and just cover with boiling water. Leave to stand for 30 minutes. Place the aubergine, potato, carrot and peas in a saucepan with 250 ml (10 fl oz) boiling water. Cover and cook for 10 minutes until vegetables are tender. Meanwhile, fry the onion and garlic in the oil for 5 minutes before adding the balti paste and tomato purée. Stir-fry for 2 minutes. Add the cooked vegetables to the onion mixture and simmer fc. 5 minutes. Mix the almonds with the coconut and add the nut mixture with the cream to the vegetables. Stir and cook gently for a few minutes to heat through. Serve.

Lasagne
Serves 4–8

> 1 aubergine, sliced
> 4 tablespoons (60 ml) oil
> 100 g (4 oz) split red lentils
> 2 red onions, chopped
> 2 cloves garlic, crushed
> 1 red pepper, chopped
> 200 g (8 oz) mushrooms, sliced
> 400-g can chopped tomatoes
> 1 tablespoon (15 ml) tomato purée
> sprinkling oregano
> salt and pepper
> 9 sheets lasagne
> 400 ml (16 fl oz) cheese sauce (see page 87)
> 25 g (1 oz) Parmesan cheese
> 50 g (2 oz) cheese, grated

Pre-heat the grill. Brush the aubergine with some of the oil and grill until brown. Turn over and repeat. Pre-heat the oven to 180°C/350°F/Gas 4. Put the lentils in a pan with just enough water to cover, boil for 10 minutes, then simmer for a further 5, topping up with boiling water as necessary. Fry the onions, garlic and pepper in the oil for 5 minutes. Add the mushrooms and cook for 5 minutes before adding the tomatoes and tomato purée. Sprinkle with oregano and simmer for 5 minutes. Mix the drained lentils and vegetables together. Season. Put a layer of the vegetable mixture in a lasagne dish. Cover with 3 sheets of lasagne and then put a third of the cheese sauce over these. Repeat the process twice to use up all the ingredients. Sprinkle with both cheeses and bake for 35 minutes.

Cheese sauce
Makes 500 ml (1 pint)

To make 400 ml (16 fl oz) for baking with, use only 350 ml (14 fl oz) milk to make a much thicker sauce.

    50 g (2 oz) butter or margarine
    50 g (2 oz) flour, sifted
    450 ml (18 fl oz) milk
    100 g (4 oz) grated cheese
    mustard to taste

Melt the butter or margarine in a small saucepan and then remove from the heat. Add the flour, stir well and return to a gentle heat, stirring continuously. Add a little milk at a time, and keep stirring to keep lumps at bay. The mixture will be very thick at first – keep thinning it gradually with the milk. When all the milk has been added, keep stirring and cooking for 2 minutes. Add the cheese and mustard, and continue cooking until cheese has melted.

Cream sauce
Omit the cheese and mustard and add a 125-ml carton double cream. Season well with plenty of black pepper.

Mushroom sauce
Omit the cheese and mustard. Add 200 g (8 oz) sliced fried mushrooms and 2 tablespoons (30 ml) double cream.

Moussaka
Serves 4

2 aubergines, sliced
6 tablespoons (90 ml) oil
2 onions, chopped
2 cloves garlic, crushed
400 g (1 lb) mushrooms, chopped
600-g can chopped tomatoes
3 tablespoons (45 ml) tomato purée
sprinkling oregano or mixed herbs
salt and pepper
2 eggs, beaten
200 g Greek yoghurt
125 g (5 oz) cheese, grated

Pre-heat the grill. Brush the aubergine slices with some of the oil. Grill until brown (about 4–5 minutes), turn over and repeat. (You may need to do this in batches if you have a small grill.) Pre-heat the oven to 200°C/400°F/Gas 6. Fry the onion and garlic in 1 tablespoon (15 ml) oil for 5–10 minutes until starting to brown. In another pan fry the mushrooms in 1 tablespoon (15 ml) oil until soft. When fried vegetables are ready, combine in one saucepan with the tomatoes, tomato purée and herbs and season with salt and pepper. Simmer for 10 minutes. Into a lasagne dish put half the vegetable mixture and cover with half of the aubergine slices. Top with the rest of the vegetable mixture and the remaining aubergine slices. Beat together the eggs, yoghurt and cheese, spoon over the aubergine slices. Cook for about 30 minutes until brown on top.

Goulash (by-election slops)
Serves 4–6

This is one of those classic student dishes that is trotted out time and time again as it is easy to make and also cheap to serve to large numbers of people. The reason for the title is that I first experienced it when we were having a late-night meal while waiting for some important by-election results. Strangely, I don't remember anything about the by-election, just the meal. This goulash was followed by extremely, and I do mean extremely, runny brie!

1.25 kg (3 lb) mixed vegetables, such as carrots,
     courgettes, potatoes, aubergines, mushrooms, corn
2 onions, chopped
2 cloves garlic, crushed
3 tablespoons (45 ml) oil
400-g can chopped tomatoes
1 red and 1 green pepper, chopped
4 tablespoons (60 ml) tomato purée
2 tablespoons (30 ml) paprika
salt and pepper

Pre-heat the oven to 190°C/375°/Gas 5. Cut the vegetables into bite-sized pieces. Fry the onion and garlic in oil for 5 minutes. Mix in the remaining ingredients and seasonings and transfer to a casserole dish. Bake for 40 minutes or until all the vegetables are cooked.

Cassoulet (mean beans)
Serves 4

This recipe from *Mean Beans* is still going down a treat with us and other garlic fiends. We usually accompany it with . . . garlic bread! This is not a dish to serve to: a) vampires, b) people who don't like garlic, or c) people about to go out for a night on the town.

2 onions, chopped
4 cloves garlic, crushed
3 tablespoons (45 ml) oil
2 x 400-g can cannellini beans, drained
2 tablespoons (30 ml) soft brown sugar
2 tablespoons (30 ml) wine vinegar
1 tablespoon (15 ml) treacle
1 tablespoon (15 ml) mustard
1 teaspoon (5 ml) chilli powder

Mean butter
2 tablespoons (30 ml) butter, softened
2 tablespoons (30 ml) French mustard
2 tablespoons (30 ml) fresh parsley, chopped
2 cloves garlic, crushed

Pre-heat the oven to 180°C/350°F/Gas 4. Fry the onions and garlic in the oil for 10 minutes. Put with the remaining ingredients (except for those for mean butter) into a casserole dish and pour in 250 ml (10 fl oz) boiling water. Do not cover. Cook for 1 hour. Just before serving, mix mean butter ingredients together and stir into beans.

Sue's chilli
Serves 5–6

My memories of the origins of this dish are vague. I do know it had something to do with watching a horse race – the Grand National? – but all I really remember is we sat on the floor with a large saucepan in the middle, helping ourselves and smothering the chilli in sour cream and tortilla chips.

1 large onion, chopped
2 cloves garlic, crushed
1 aubergine, diced
1 green pepper, diced
2 carrots, sliced
150 g (6 oz) mushrooms, sliced
2 x 400-g can tomatoes
oil for frying
2 x 400-g can beans in chilli sauce
3 tablespoons (45 ml) tomato purée
1–3 teaspoons (5–15 ml) chilli powder, to taste
salt and pepper

Fry the vegetables in a little oil until soft. Heat up the beans in a large saucepan and add the vegetables and tomato purée. Season and simmer gently for 30 minutes. Serve with pitta bread, sour cream and tortilla chips.

Chilli sin carne
Serves 4

1 onion, chopped
1 clove garlic, crushed
1 green pepper, chopped
2 tablespoons (30 ml) oil
250 g minced Quorn
2 tablespoons (30 ml) tomato purée
400-g can chopped tomatoes
400-g can red kidney beans, drained
1 packet Old El Paso chilli mix

Fry the onion, garlic and pepper in the oil until soft. Add Quorn and continue to cook until brown. Add the remaining ingredients and mix well. Cover tightly and simmer gently for 15 minutes.

Pizza
Serves 2–

1 quantity pizza dough (see page 50)
1 quantity tomato sauce (see page 51)
few thin slices green pepper
few thin slices red pepper
50 g (2 oz) mushrooms, chopped
2 spring onions, sliced
50 g (2 oz) mozzarella cheese, grated
salt and pepper
sprinkling chilli flakes

Pre-heat the oven to 200°C/400°F/Gas 6. Roll the dough out into a 30-cm (12-in) circle. Place on a large baking sheet. Prick all over with a fork. Spread with tomato sauce. Arrange vegetables on top and sprinkle with the cheese. Season to taste with salt, pepper and chilli flakes. Cook for 25–35 minutes.

6 Dinner Parties

Although this is not an aspect of cooking that people generally consider when they think of student cooking, it is something that some students find very enjoyable. You don't have to be a gourmet chef to be able to cook for these dinner parties. These are tried and tested recipes which even those who have little experience can undertake. The menus I have chosen are varied and mirror meals that one would generally enjoy in restaurants – but at a fraction of the cost.

Organisation is the key to happy entertaining; check and double-check! Be particularly wary of assuming that you have an ingredient in your store cupboard only to discover at the last minute that what you actually have is an empty container.

I have arranged this chapter to make it as easy as possible for you. For each menu I have worked out a shopping list and a time plan. Just remember: a) if you are providing the drinks you need to add these to your shopping list (ditto coffee/milk if you are having them); b) the time plan is the preparation time *after* you have got everything ready, that is, chopped the vegetables, pre-cooked items, etc. Only you can estimate how long that will take you.

Menu 1

Garlic mushrooms
Stuffed aubergines
Brown rice
Salad
Squidgy tart
Preparation time: 1 hour

Shopping list

375 g (15 oz) mushrooms
5 cloves garlic
3 aubergines
2 red onions
80–100 g pack of salad leaves
75 g (3 oz) green lentils
300 g (12 oz) easy cook brown rice
wine *or* sherry vinegar
olive oil
tomato purée

dried herbs
French mustard
100 g (4 oz) good cooking chocolate
200 g (8 oz) tiny marshmallows
1 sweet pastry shell
French bread
wine (optional)
250-ml carton double cream
75 g (3 oz) butter
salt and pepper

Time plan: to eat at 8:30

7.30   Make squidgy tart
7.40   Mix vinaigrette ingredients together
7.45   Prepare stuffed aubergines
8.20   Start garlic mushrooms
8.30   Put rice on to cook
        Put aubergines in oven
        Serve garlic mushrooms
Later: Dress salad just before serving

Garlic mushrooms
Serves 6

This is my latest version of garlic mushrooms. I have started adding cream to this dish and I do think that this makes it even nicer. (Yes – and even more fattening. But as long as you don't eat it every day it won't hurt.)

300 g (12 oz) mushrooms, quartered
3 cloves garlic, crushed
75 g (3 oz) butter
6 slices French bread
1½ teaspoons (7.5 ml) French mustard
3 tablespoons (45 ml) double cream

Pre-heat grill. Cook mushrooms and garlic in butter for 3 minutes. Toast bread. Add French mustard and cream to mushroom mixture, heat through and serve on the toasted bread.

Stuffed aubergines
Serves 6

> 75 g (3 oz) green lentils
> 2 red onions, chopped
> 2 cloves garlic, crushed
> 75 g (3 oz) mushrooms, sliced
> 5 tablespoons (75 ml) olive oil
> 3 tablespoons (45 ml) tomato purée
> 5 tablespoons (75 ml) red wine *or* water
> 3 aubergines, halved and flesh scooped out and diced
> salt and pepper

Pre-heat oven to 200°C/400°F/Gas 6. Boil lentils in plenty of water for 10 minutes and then simmer for a further 20. Meanwhile, fry the onions, garlic and mushrooms in one-third of the oil, until starting to brown. Remove from pan. Reserve 1 tablespoon oil and 1 tablespoon tomato purée, heat the rest of the oil and then cook the aubergine for 5 minutes. Return other vegetables to pan and add tomato purée and wine (or water). Stir and then remove from heat. Season well. When lentils are cooked add to other ingredients. Use to stuff the aubergine shells. Mix reserved oil and tomato purée and brush over shell edges. Place on a baking tray and bake for 25 minutes.

Brown rice
Serves 6

> 300 g (12 oz) easy cook brown rice

Put rice in a large saucepan with 750 ml (1½ pints) cold water. Cover and bring to the boil. Stir and replace lid. Simmer for 20–25 minutes, until all water is absorbed.

Salad
Serves 6

    80–100 g pack of salad leaves

    Vinaigrette
    3 tablespoons (45 ml) olive oil
    1 tablespoon (15 ml) wine *or* sherry vinegar
    pinch dried herbs
    salt and pepper

Mix all vinaigrette ingredients together and use to dress salad.
Serve immediately.

Squidgy tart
Serves 6

This is not a recipe for a strict vegetarian because if you look
carefully at the ingredients on the marshmallow pack you will
find gelatin. This came as a complete surprise to me, as I'd
never suspected marshmallows of not being suitable for
vegetarians. It just shows how careful you have to be if you are
determined to exclude animal products completely from your
diet.

    125-ml carton double cream
    100 g (4 oz) good cooking chocolate
    200 g (8 oz) tiny marshmallows
    1 sweet pastry shell

Put the double cream, chocolate and half the marshmallows
into a saucepan, heat gently, stirring until melted. Pour into
pastry shell, top with remaining marshmallows. Chill.

Menu 2

Potato skins and sour cream dip
Vegeburgers
Oven chips
Salad with banana dressing
Ice-cream with chocolate fudge sauce
Preparation time: 1 hour

Shopping list

4 x 250 g (10 oz) potatoes
chives
punnet mustard and cress
1 clove garlic (optional)
packet mixed lettuce leaves
1 white or red cabbage
1 yellow pepper
1 banana
oil
soy sauce
chilli powder

salt and pepper
jar chilli relish
white wine vinegar
honey
soft brown sugar
125-ml carton sour cream
butter
4 chargrilled vegeburgers
500 ml vanilla ice-cream
4 sesame seed burger buns
1 65-g Mars bar

Time plan: to eat at 8:30

7.30 Measure out ingredients for fudge sauce
      Prepare salad and dressing (but don't add banana until
      you are ready to serve)
7.40 Prepare potato skins
      Pre-heat oven
7.50 Prepare oven chips
8.10 Put potato skins in oven
      Prepare dip
8.20 Put oven chips in oven
8.30 Turn down oven temperature
      Put in vegeburgers
      Serve potato skins and dip
8.50 Serve main course

Potato skins
Serves 4

4 x 250 g (10 oz) potatoes
2 tablespoons (30 ml) oil
2 tablespoons (30 ml) soy sauce
pinch chilli powder

Pre-heat the oven to 220°C/425°F/Gas 7. Cut the skins from the potatoes thickly (the flesh will be used for the oven chips). Mix with the other ingredients. Put on a baking tray and cook for about 20 minutes until crisp and brown. Serve with the dip (below).

Sour cream dip
Serves 4

125-ml carton sour cream
2 tablespoons (30 ml) chopped chives
salt and pepper
1 clove garlic, crushed (optional)

Combine all ingredients, and pour into a small serving bowl.

Vegeburgers
Serves 4

I have never been that impressed with the vegeburgers that we have tried. Many are fairly tasteless and, even worse, tend to fall apart when you cook them. However, the chargrilled vegeburgers that you can buy in Safeways are the exception. We have been really impressed with both their flavour and their texture. Well worth hunting out.

    4 chargrilled vegeburgers
    4 sesame seed burger buns
    3 tablespoons (45 ml) chilli relish

Pre-heat oven to 180°C/350°F/Gas 4. Place burgers on a baking tray and cook for 20 minutes, turning once. Split buns in half. When burgers are cooked, put one on each bun, top with chilli relish and cover with remaining bun halves. Serve immediately.

Oven chips
Serves 4

    4 x 250 g (10 oz) potatoes, skins removed
    2 tablespoons (30 ml) oil
    salt

Pre-heat oven to 220°C/425°F/Gas 7. Cut potatoes into slices and then cut the slices into strips. Put into a saucepan with cold water and bring to the boil. Cook for 3 minutes then plunge potatoes into cold water. Drain and pat dry. Mix with oil and season with salt. Place on a baking tray and cook for 10 minutes. Then turn down heat to 180°C/350°F/Gas 5 and bake for a further 20–25 minutes until chips have browned.

Salad with banana dressing
Serves 4

> packet mixed lettuce leaves
> 100 g (4 oz) white or red cabbage, thinly sliced
> 1 yellow pepper, chopped
> punnet mustard and cress
>
> *Banana dressing*
> 4 tablespoons (60 ml) oil
> 1 tablespoon (15 ml) white wine vinegar
> 1 teaspoon (5 ml) honey
> 1 banana, chopped finely
> salt and pepper

Place salad ingredients in a serving bowl. Combine all dressing ingredients thoroughly and pour over salad. Toss and serve immediately.

Ice-cream with chocolate fudge sauce
Serves 4

This is utterly delicious and very popular in our household.

> 1 65-g Mars bar, chopped
> 1 tablespoon (15 ml) butter
> 1 tablespoon (15 ml) soft brown sugar
> 500 ml vanilla ice-cream

Place a heat-proof bowl over a small saucepan of boiling water. (Don't let it touch the water.) Put the Mars bar, butter and sugar in the bowl to melt. Then beat in 1 tablespoon (15 ml) boiling water. When the sauce is smooth, pour over the ice-cream and serve.

Menu 3

Crudités with garlic dip
Fajitas
Salad, sour cream, grated cheese
Salsa
Guacamole
Chocolate tiramisu
Preparation time: 1 hour

Shopping list

2 carrots
2 green peppers
2 red peppers
½ cucumber
½ cauliflower
6 cloves garlic
1 red onion
3 tomatoes
1 aubergine
1 small onion
1 lemon
1 large ripe avocado
salad leaves
soft cream cheese
125-ml carton single cream
125-ml carton sour cream

100 g (4 oz) grated cheese
250 g mascarpone cheese
eggs
mayonnaise
oil
chilli powder
ground coriander
8 tortillas
caster sugar
vanilla essence
coffee
230-g can chopped tomatoes
tomato purée
miniature brandy
2 chocolate flakes
box sponge fingers

Time plan: to eat at 8:30

7.30   Prepare tiramisu
7.40   Prepare salsa
7.50   Prepare crudités
7.55   Prepare dip
8.00   Prepare guacamole
8.05   Prepare stuffing for tortillas (keep warm)
8.30   Serve crudités and dip
8.50   Serve main course

Crudités
Serves 4

2 carrots, cut into matchsticks
1 red pepper, cut into lengths
½ cucumber, cut in half and then into lengths
½ small cauliflower, divided into florets

After you have prepared the vegetables, store them in a plastic bag in the salad drawer of the fridge to keep fresh. When ready to eat, serve with garlic dip.

Garlic dip
Serves 4

2 tablespoons (30 ml) soft cream cheese
2 tablespoons (30 ml) single cream
2 tablespoons (30 ml) mayonnaise
2 cloves garlic, crushed

Mix all ingredients together thoroughly.

Cheese dip
Serves 4

If you want to serve different dips, remember to adjust your shopping list accordingly.

125 g soft cream cheese
1 tablespoon (15 ml) soft margarine or butter
1 tablespoon (15 ml) mayonnaise

Blend together the cheese and margarine, and then stir in the mayonnaise.

Blue cheese dip
To the above, add some crushed blue cheese, such as Danish blue.

Cheese and tomato dip
To the main recipe, add 1 tablespoon (15 ml) tomato ketchup or purée.

Tomato and garlic dip
Serves 4

2 tablespoons (30 ml) tomato purée
1 tablespoon (15 ml) oil
2 cloves garlic, crushed
salt and pepper

Mix all ingredients together thoroughly with 2 tablespoons (30 ml) hot water.

Fajitas
Serves 4

    8 tablespoons (120 ml) oil
    2 cloves garlic, crushed
    1 aubergine, thinly sliced
    1 red onion, sliced
    1 red pepper, diced
    1 green pepper, diced
    2 tomatoes, skinned (see page 56) and chopped
    sprinkling chilli powder
    pinch ground coriander
    8 tortillas

Mix together 6 tablespoons (90 ml) of the oil and the garlic. Use to coat the aubergines and grill until brown. (Takes about 4–5 minutes each side.) Fry the onion and peppers in the rest of the oil for 5 minutes. Then add the tomatoes, chilli and coriander and fry for a further 5 minutes. Mix all the vegetables together and use as a stuffing for the tortillas.

    Fajitas are usually served with salad, grated cheese, sour cream and salsa.

Salsa
Serves 4–6

Although you can now buy many varieties of salsa in the shops and some of them are very good, I still like to make my own. You can alter the heat of your salsa by varying the amount of chilli you use. You can also use chilli sauce rather than chilli powder if you prefer.

> ½ green pepper, finely chopped
> 1 small onion, finely chopped
> 2 tablespoons (30 ml) oil
> 2 cloves garlic, crushed
> sprinkling chilli powder
> 230-g can chopped tomatoes
> 1 tablespoon (15 ml) tomato purée

Fry the pepper and onion in 1 tablespoon (15 ml) of the oil for 5 minutes. Add the garlic, chilli and tomatoes and simmer gently for 5 minutes. Finally, add the rest of the oil and the tomato purée, stir and leave to cool.

Guacamole
Serves 4–6

In our house this is a very popular dish. I often serve it with salsa and a sour cream dip and crudités and tortilla chips. My recipe often changes; this is the one we are using at the moment.

> 1 large ripe avocado, peeled and stored
> ½ teaspoon (2.5 ml) tomato purée *or* 1 chopped tomato
> sprinkling chilli or cayenne pepper
> squeeze fresh lemon juice

Mash the avocado flesh to a smooth purée and then mix with remaining ingredients. Serve with crudités or tortilla chips.

Chocolate tiramisu
Serves 4–6

250 g mascarpone cheese
2 egg yolks, beaten
2 tablespoons (30 ml) caster sugar
1 teaspoon (5 ml) vanilla essence
200 ml (8 fl oz) double-strength black coffee
miniature brandy
box sponge fingers
2 chocolate flakes, crumbled

Beat together the mascarpone cheese, egg yolks, caster sugar and vanilla essence. Mix together the coffee and brandy. Dip half the sponge fingers into the coffee mixture and arrange in a serving dish. Cover with half the mascarpone mixture and half the chocolate flake. Dip the remaining fingers in the coffee and arrange in another layer on top. Cover with the rest of the mascarpone mixture and sprinkle the rest of the chocolate over it. Chill before serving.

Menu 4

Pakoras
Mint, coconut and coriander rata
Bean dhansak
Mushroom and coriander bhajee
Bhindi bhajee (okra curry)
Lemon rice
Mango cream
Preparation time: 1½ hours

Shopping list

1 cauliflower
1 pepper
15 g packet mint leaves
2 x 15 g packet coriander
  leaves
2 lemons
spring onions
7 cloves garlic
400 g (1 lb) okra
400 g (1 lb) mushrooms
1 aubergine
1 potato
200 g (8 oz) carrots
4 onions
150-ml carton natural
  yoghurt
250-ml carton double cream

desiccated coconut
150 g (6 oz) basmati rice
plain flour
salt
garam masala
ginger purée
curry paste
balti paste
turmeric
oil
tomato purée
600-g can chopped tomatoes
200-g can chopped tomatoes
400-g can red kidney beans
split red lentils
vegetable stock cube
400-g can mango slices

Time plan: to eat at 8:30

7.00	Soak coconut for raita
7.05	Make mango cream
7.15	Make raita
7.25	Start bhindi bhajee
	Pre-heat to 150°C/300°F/Gas 2 to keep dishes warm as you cook them
7.35	Start bean dhansak
7.50	Start mushroom and coriander bhajee
8.05	Start cooking rice
8.10	Start making pakoras
8.30	Serve pakoras with raita
8.45	Serve main course

Pakoras
Serves 4

100 g (4 oz) plain flour
pinch salt
oil for frying
1 teaspoon (5 ml) garam masala
6–8 cauliflower florets, halved
1 pepper, sliced into rings

Blend the flour and salt with just enough water (about 125 ml (5 fl oz)) to make a smooth batter. Pour enough oil into a pan to give a depth of 2.5 cm (1 in) and heat until very hot. Dip vegetables into batter and then fry a few pieces at a time for 5–6 minutes until golden brown.

Mint, coconut and coriander raita
Serves 4

2 tablespoons (30 ml) desiccated coconut
15 g packet mint leaves, chopped
15 g packet coriander leaves, chopped (but reserve
    1 tablespoon for the bhindi bhajee)
2–3 spring onions, chopped
1 clove garlic, crushed
1 teaspoon (5 ml) ginger purée
2 teaspoons (10 ml) curry paste
4 tablespoons (60 ml) yoghurt

Mix the coconut with 3 tablespoons (45 ml) boiling water and leave to soak for 15 minutes. Add the other ingredients, stir thoroughly and chill before serving.

Bean dhansak
Serves 4

1 aubergine (200 g/8 oz), diced
1 potato (200 g/8 oz), cut into matchsticks
200 g (8 oz) carrots, diced
1 onion, sliced
2 cloves garlic, crushed
3 tablespoons (45 ml) oil
200 g (8 oz) mushrooms, sliced
1 teaspoon (5 ml) ginger purée
2 tablespoons (30 ml) balti paste
2 tablespoons (30 ml) tomato purée
100 g (4 oz) split red lentils
600-g can chopped tomatoes
400-g can red kidney beans, drained

Cook the aubergine, potato and carrot in boiling water for 10 minutes, then drain. Fry the onion and garlic in 2 tablespoons (30 ml) oil for 5 minutes until soft. Add the remaining oil and the mushrooms and continue to cook for 5 minutes. Add the ginger, balti paste and tomato purée. Fry for 3 minutes. Meanwhile, cook the lentils for 10 minutes in just enough boiling water to cover, topping up with water as necessary. Transfer all ingredients except beans to a large saucepan. Bring to the boil, cover and simmer for 15 minutes. Then add beans and simmer for a further 5 minutes. Serve.

Mushroom and coriander bhajee
Serves 4

1 onion, chopped
3 tablespoons (45 ml) oil
2 teaspoons (10 ml) garam masala
2 cloves garlic, crushed
1 tablespoon (15 ml) tomato purée
200 g (8 oz) mushrooms, sliced
15 g packet coriander, chopped

Fry the onion for 5 minutes in the oil, add the garam masala and garlic and cook for a further 2 minutes. Add the tomato purée and mushrooms and stir-fry for 4–5 minutes until mushrooms are cooked. Add the coriander and stir before serving.

Bhindi bhajee (okra curry)
Serves 4

450 g (1 lb) okra, topped and tailed
2 onions, chopped
2 cloves garlic, crushed
6 tablespoons (90 ml) oil
1 teaspoon (5 ml) ginger purée
2 tablespoons (30 ml) balti paste
200-g can chopped tomatoes
1 tablespoon (15 ml) tomato purée
1 tablespoon (15 ml) fresh coriander, chopped

Fry the okra, onions and garlic in the oil for 5 minutes. Add ginger and curry paste and cook for 3 minutes. Add tomatoes and tomato purée. Cover and cook for 15 minutes. Stir in the coriander and serve.

Lemon rice
Serves 4

    1 teaspoon (5 ml) turmeric
    1 tablespoon (15 ml) oil
    2 lemons, rind of
    150 g (6 oz) basmati rice
    375 ml (15 fl oz) vegetable stock

Fry the turmeric in the oil for 1 minute, add the lemon rind and the rice and stir. Pour in the vegetable stock, bring to the boil, cover and simmer for 10–12 minutes until rice is cooked.

Mango cream
Serves 4

    400-g can mango slices, drained
    250-ml carton double cream

Mash the mango slices to a smooth purée. Lightly whip the cream until it starts to hold its shape. Mix the mango purée and cream together, and pour into 4 small serving dishes. Chill.

Menu 5

Sweet 'n' sour vegetables
Tomato and chilli chow mein
Stir-fried broccoli and cashews
Egg fried rice
Lychees and mangoes
Preparation time: 30 minutes

Shopping list

1 green pepper
1 red pepper
1 carrot
2 sticks celery
100 g (4 oz) mushrooms
200 g (8 oz) broccoli
1 clove garlic
frozen peas
300 g (12 oz) rice
oil
soy sauce
chilli sauce
tomato sauce

Chinese nest noodles
225-g can bamboo shoots
160-g jar sweet 'n' sour sauce
410-g can mangoes
425-g can lychees
50 g (2 oz) unsalted cashews
ginger purée
sherry or white wine
cornflour
honey
1 egg
salt and pepper

Time plan: to eat at 8:30

8.00 Pre-heat oven to 150°C/300°F/Gas 2 to keep dishes
warm as you cook them
Prepare lychees and mangoes
Put rice on to cook
8.10 Prepare sweet 'n' sour vegetables
8.15 Prepare stir-fried broccoli and cashews
Prepare noodles for chow mein
8.20 Prepare egg fried rice
8.25 Prepare tomato and chilli chow mein
8.30 Serve

Sweet 'n' sour vegetables
Serves 4

1 green pepper, sliced
1 red pepper, sliced
1 carrot, cut into matchsticks
2 sticks celery, sliced
2 tablespoons (30 ml) oil
225-g can bamboo shoots, drained
160-g jar sweet 'n' sour sauce

Stir-fry the peppers, carrot and celery in the oil for 2–3 minutes. Add the bamboo shoots and sweet 'n' sour sauce. Cook for 2 minutes and serve.

Tomato and chilli chow mein
Serves 4

100 g (4 oz) Chinese nest noodles
2 tablespoons (30 ml) oil
100 g (4 oz) mushrooms
50 g (2 oz) frozen peas

Sauce
2 tablespoons (30 ml) soy sauce
1 tablespoon (15 ml) chilli sauce
2 tablespoons (30 ml) tomato sauce

Cook the noodles until soft. Drain. Toss in 1 tablespoon oil. Stir-fry the mushrooms and peas in the remaining oil for 2 minutes. Pour in the sauce ingredients and cook for 1 minute. Add the noodles and stir through before serving.

Stir-fried broccoli and cashews
Serves 4

200 g (8 oz) broccoli florets, sliced
1 clove garlic, crushed
1 teaspoon (5 ml) ginger purée
1 tablespoon (15 ml) oil
50 g (2 oz) unsalted cashews

Sauce
1 teaspoon (5 ml) cornflour
2 tablespoons (30 ml) soy sauce
2 tablespoons (30 ml) sherry or white wine
1 teaspoon (5 ml) honey

Stir-fry the broccoli, garlic and ginger in the oil for 2 minutes. Add the cashews and stir through. Dissolve the cornflour in 4 tablespoons (60 ml) of water. Mix with the other sauce ingredients and add to the pan. Cook for 2 minutes. Serve.

Egg fried rice
Serves 4

300 g (12 oz) cooked rice
2 tablespoons (30 ml) oil
1 egg, lightly beaten
salt and pepper

Stir-fry the rice in the oil, add the egg and continue to stir until egg starts to set. Season well and serve.

Lychees and mangoes
Serves 4

425-g can lychees
410-g can mangoes

Drain both cans, reserving 4 tablespoons (60 ml) syrup from can of mangoes. Divide fruit between 4 serving bowls and spoon some of the reserved juice over each. Serve.

7 Feeding the Loved One

These are recipes for those romantic *dîners à deux* to celebrate birthdays, Valentine's Day and other special occasions. You can also prepare them when you are trying to attract that special person into your life. Whether you go to town on the presentation – flowers, candles, etc. – depends on your own style and on how obvious you want your intentions to be!

If using wine in cooking you could get a measure from the student bar or a can from a supermarket or off-licence. The cans hold two measures (one for the dish, one for the cook!) This saves you having to open a bottle – which you would probably rather drink, or which could be difficult if it is your guest who is bringing the wine.

Menu 1

Pasta with walnuts
Side salad
Ricotta with honey and pine-nuts
Preparation time: 20 minutes

Shopping list

100 g (4 oz) mushrooms
1 little gem lettuce
1 iceberg lettuce
bunch of spring onions
bunch of radishes
½ cucumber
1 clove garlic
pine-nuts
50 g (2 oz) chopped walnuts
150 g (6 oz) pasta bows *or*
   tagliatelle

butter
80 g Boursin
250-g tub ricotta cheese
milk
salt and pepper
oil
wine vinegar
dried mustard powder
runny honey

Order of cooking

1. Prepare ricotta (do not sprinkle with nuts)
2. Prepare salad and dressing
3. Prepare and cook pasta
4. Dress salad and serve with pasta
5. Sprinkle ricotta with pine-nuts and serve

Pasta with walnuts
Serves 2

150 g (6 oz) pasta bows *or* tagliatelle
100 g (4 oz) mushrooms, sliced
25 g (1 oz) butter
80 g Boursin, garlic and herb flavoured
4 tablespoons (60 ml) milk
50 g (2 oz) chopped walnuts
salt and pepper

Cook the pasta as directed on the packet. Meanwhile, fry the mushrooms in the butter for 2–3 minutes. Add the Boursin and milk to the pan and gently melt down to make a sauce. Add the walnuts and heat through. Season well and serve with the pasta.

Side salad
Serves 2

1 little gem lettuce, shredded
few slices iceberg lettuce
2–3 spring onions, sliced
3–4 radishes, sliced
7-cm (3-inch) length of cucumber, sliced

Dressing
2 tablespoons (30 ml) oil
2 teaspoons (10 ml) wine vinegar
1 clove garlic, crushed
pinch salt
pinch dried mustard powder

Place salad ingredients in a bowl. Mix dressing ingredients together and pour over salad just before serving.

Ricotta with honey and pine-nuts
Serves 2

> 3 teaspoons (15 ml) runny honey
> 250-g tub ricotta cheese
> 1 tablespoon (15 ml) pine-nuts

Mix 2 teaspoons (10 ml) of the honey with the cheese and then divide between two bowls. Drizzle the remaining honey over the ricotta and sprinkle with the nuts.

Menu 2

Sweet aubergine stew
Buttered rice
Raspberry creams
Preparation time: 1 hour

Shopping list

1 red onion
1 clove garlic
200 g (8 oz) mushrooms
1 red pepper
1 aubergine
100 g (4 oz) raspberries
oil
125-ml carton whipping
   cream

butter
100 g (4 oz) basmati rice
lemon *or* ginger crisp biscuits
400-g can chopped tomatoes
soft light brown sugar
red wine
salt and pepper

Order of cooking

1. Prepare and cook aubergine stew
2. Prepare raspberry creams
3. Soak basmati rice
4. 20 minutes before you wish to eat, cook rice

Sweet aubergine stew
Serves 2

 1 red onion, chopped
 1 clove garlic, crushed
 200 g (8 oz) mushrooms, quartered
 1 red pepper, diced
 2 tablespoons (30 ml) oil
 200 g (8 oz) aubergine, diced
 400-g can chopped tomatoes
 1 dessertspoon (10 ml) soft light brown sugar
 125 ml (5 fl oz) red wine
 salt and pepper

Pre-heat the oven to 180°C/350°F/Gas 4. Fry the onion, garlic, mushrooms and pepper in the oil for 2–3 minutes. Add the aubergine and continue to fry for 5 minutes. Transfer to a casserole dish and add the tomatoes, sugar and red wine. Season. Cover and cook for 50 minutes.

Buttered rice
Serves 2

 100 g (4 oz) basmati rice
 25 g (1 oz) butter

Place the rice and half the butter in a pan with 250 ml (½ pint) cold water. Bring to the boil, stir and cover. Simmer for 10–12 minutes until water is absorbed. Fork remaining butter into rice before serving.

Raspberry creams
Serves 2

> 100 g (4 oz) raspberries
> 125-ml carton whipping cream
> lemon *or* ginger crisp biscuits (to serve)

Mash or purée the fruit – or sieve if preferred. I like the texture you get when the fruit is just mashed. Whip the cream until it holds its shape. Gently stir in the fruit and divide between 2 bowls. Serve with some crisp lemon or ginger biscuits.

Menu 3

Crunchy stuffed courgettes
Creamy potatoes
Steamed broccoli
Strawberries and cream
Preparation time: 35 minutes

Shopping list

2 large courgettes
1 onion
100 g (4 oz) mushrooms
200 g (8 oz) new potatoes
200 g (8 oz) punnet
   strawberries
200 g (8 oz) broccoli
oil
tomato purée

white wine *or* sherry
dried tarragon
roasted chopped hazelnuts
salt and pepper
butter
80 g Boursin
milk
150-ml carton single cream

Order of cooking

1. Prepare and cook crunchy stuffed courgettes
2. Cook creamy potatoes
3. Prepare strawberries
4. Cook broccoli (over potatoes)

Crunchy stuffed courgettes
Serves 2

2 large courgettes
1 tablespoon (15 ml) oil
½ onion, finely chopped
100 g (4 oz) mushrooms, finely chopped
1 dessertspoon (10 ml) tomato purée
1 tablespoon (15 ml) white wine *or* sherry
sprinkling dried tarragon
salt and pepper
25 g (1 oz) roasted chopped hazelnuts

Pre-heat the oven to 190°C/375°F/Gas 5. Cut each courgette in half lengthways. Carefully score a line parallel to the end of the courgette and running down each side. You can then gently spoon out the inside, leaving a boat-like shell. Chop the flesh finely and fry in the oil with the onion and mushrooms for 2–3 minutes. Add the tomato purée, the wine or sherry, the tarragon and the seasoning. Stir well and simmer gently for 2 minutes. Lay the courgette shells in a roasting tin, fill with the cooked mixture and sprinkle with the nuts. Bake for 25 minutes.

Creamy potatoes
Serves 2

200 g (8 oz) new potatoes, unpeeled
½ onion, chopped
knob of butter
80 g Boursin
4 tablespoons (60 ml) milk

Boil the potatoes until ready (approximately 15–20 minutes). Gently fry onion in butter for 2–3 minutes. Add Boursin and milk. Stir while this melts down to make a sauce. When potatoes are ready, drain and mix with sauce before serving.

Steamed broccoli
Serves 2

200 g (8 oz) broccoli florets

Place broccoli in a steamer or metal colander over a pan of boiling water. Cover and cook for 8 minutes.

Strawberries and cream
Serves 2

200 g (8 oz) punnet strawberries
150-ml carton single cream

Hull strawberries and cut each in half (unless they are very small, in which case they can be left whole). Divide between two bowls and serve cream separately.

8 Sweet Things

Everyone likes a treat now and again. Although students do not often bother with desserts, occasionally you will want to indulge yourself. These recipes are very easy to make – in fact I like to think they are foolproof, although I know there are those who somehow will manage to go astray . . . Everyone has a disaster some time. A friend recently reminded me of the occasion when I made a cake which came out flat as a pancake – I had forgotten to put in the flour! And not so long ago we waited rather a long time for a cake to cook, as someone (who shall remain nameless) hadn't turned the oven on!

I fondly remember the pancake parties that one of our friends used to give. He was an absolute ace at pancakes and provided lots of scrummy fillings. As long as we kept him supplied with drinks, he kept us supplied with pancakes. We helped ourselves as the pancakes arrived – and just kept going until we were in danger of bursting!

Banana Hobnob crunch
Serves 1

>   1 small banana, mashed
>   100-g pot banana fromage frais
>   2 chocolate Hobnob biscuits, crumbled

Mix together the banana purée and the fromage frais. Layer the banana mixture and the biscuit crumbs into a small bowl, finishing with a layer of crumbs.

Pancakes
Serves 2–3

>   100 g (4 oz) flour
>   pinch of salt
>   1 egg, beaten
>   250 ml (10 fl oz) milk
>   oil *or* butter for frying
>   sugar (for serving)
>   lemon (for serving)

Sift the flour and salt into a bowl. Make a well in the middle and pour the egg and half the milk into it. Beat together well, gradually adding more milk until you have a smoother thin batter. Heat a little oil or butter in a small frying pan and ladle in just enough pancake mixture to cover the bottom of the pan. Cook until the bottom of the pancake starts to brown (lift pancake at the edge to check). Flip(!) the pancake over and cook the other side for a minute or two. Slide on to a serving plate and sprinkle with sugar and a squeeze of lemon.

Baked apples
Serves 4

> 4 large Bramley apples, cored
> 3 tablespoons (45 ml) mincemeat

Pre-heat the oven to 180°C/350°F/Gas 4. Score around the middle of the apples and put in a baking dish. Fill each apple cavity with the mincemeat. Pour 2 tablespoons (30 ml) water into the baking dish and cook for 45–60 minutes until apples are soft.

Mum's baked apples
My mother makes baked apples as above but uses a mixture of sultanas, butter and sugar instead of mincemeat to stuff the apples.

Danish apple pudding
Serves 4

> 1 kg (2 lb) Bramley apples, peeled and diced
> 75 g (3 oz) butter
> honey, golden syrup *or* sugar to taste
> 150 g (6 oz) fresh wholemeal breadcrumbs
> 50 g (2 oz) soft dark brown sugar

Cook the apples with 25 g (1 oz) of the butter until very soft (takes about 6–8 minutes). Mash into a purée and sweeten to taste. Leave to cool. Meanwhile, heat the remaining butter and fry the breadcrumbs with the brown sugar until they start to crisp. Leave to cool. When both purée and crumbs are cold, layer into 4 small serving bowls, alternating layers of fruit with crumbs, finishing with a layer of crumbs.

Apple crumble
Serves 4–8

    1 kg (2 lb) Bramley apples, peeled and cut into chunks
    2 tablespoons (30 ml) butter
    2 tablespoons (30 ml) caster sugar
    75 g (3 oz) self-raising wholemeal flour
    75 g (3 oz) soft dark brown sugar
    75 g (3 oz) butter, chopped

Pre-heat the oven to 200°C/400°F/Gas 6. Cook the apples with the 2 tablespoons of butter, until soft but not falling apart. Stir in the caster sugar and put in a pie dish or small casserole dish. Using your fingertips, rub together the flour, brown sugar and chopped butter until the mixture resembles breadcrumbs. Cover the fruit with the crumb mixture and bake for 30 minutes until topping begins to brown.

Plum and raisin oat-topped crumble
Serves 1–2

If the plums are not ripe enough to stone easily, stew them whole and remove the stones afterwards.

    200 g (8 oz) ripe dessert plums, halved and stoned
    1 tablespoon (15 ml) orange juice
    1 tablespoon (15 ml) sugar
    1 tablespoon (15 ml) raisins

    Crumble
    2 tablespoons (30 ml) plain wholemeal flour
    25 g (1 oz) butter *or* margarine
    1 tablespoon (15 ml) sugar
    2 tablespoons (30 ml) porridge oats

Pre-heat the oven to 200°C/400°F/Gas 6. Gently stew plums, orange juice, sugar and raisins until soft and syrupy (about 15 minutes.) Put into a small casserole or pie dish. Using your fingertips rub together the flour and butter until they resemble breadcrumbs, add sugar and oats. Cover plums with the crumble mixture. Cook for 20–25 minutes until beginning to brown.

Mummy's baked custard
Serves 2–3

You can improve the texture of your custard by placing the custard dish in a roasting tin with enough boiling water to come halfway up the dish. Then bake as below.

> 2 whole eggs and 1 yolk
> 1 tablespoon (15 ml) sugar
> few drops vanilla essence
> 250 ml (10 fl oz) milk
> grated nutmeg (optional)
> knob of butter

Pre-heat the oven to 150°C/300°F/Gas 2. Beat together the eggs, yolk, sugar and vanilla essence. Put the milk into a small saucepan and bring up to boiling point. Remove from heat immediately, pour on to egg and sugar mixture and stir well. Strain into a greased pie dish or small casserole dish and sprinkle with some grated nutmeg, if using. Put a little knob of butter on top and bake for 40–60 minutes until custard has set and a skin has formed.

Rice pudding
Serves 2–3

2 tablespoons (30 ml) pudding rice
1 tablespoon (15 ml) sugar
500 ml (1 pint) milk
knob of butter
grated nutmeg (optional)

Pre-heat the oven to 150°C/300°F/Gas 2. Put the rice, sugar and milk in a greased pie dish or small casserole dish. Top with little pieces of butter and sprinkle with grated nutmeg, if using. Bake for about 2 hours, until the rice has absorbed the milk and a skin has formed.

Greek honey-nut pie
Serves 4–6

This is an incredibly rich recipe – but utterly delicious! You must serve it in small portions and only on special occasions, as I hate to think what it does to the waistline! Sweet pastry shells can be bought in most large supermarkets and are very good (and I suspect may work out cheaper than making your own).

3 tablespoons (45 ml) caster sugar
3 tablespoons (45 ml) Greek honey
3 tablespoons (45 ml) double cream
75 g (3 oz) butter, chopped
150 g (6 oz) mixed nuts, such as pecans and hazelnuts, chopped
190-g sweet pastry shell

Pre-heat the oven to 190°C/375°F/Gas 5. In a small pan dissolve the sugar in the honey, stirring over a gentle heat, then boil for 3 minutes. Add the cream and butter and beat well. Stir in the nuts and pour into the pastry shell. Level the top and bake for 25–30 minutes.

Banofee pie
Serves 6–8

It is very important to stir all the time you are heating the toffee mixture. I had a very nasty experience once when I was so busy chatting to someone that I forgot. You will find lots of horrible burnt bits appear if you follow my example – so don't forget to keep stirring!

> 1 sweet pastry shell
> 2 bananas, mashed
> 150 g (6 oz) butter
> 2 tablespoons (30 ml) brown sugar
> 400-g can sweetened condensed milk
> aerosol can whipping cream

Cover the base of the pastry shell with the mashed banana. Melt the butter gently with the sugar. Do not boil. Add the condensed milk and bring slowly to the boil, stirring all the time. As soon as the mixture begins to bubble, turn the heat right down and simmer gently for a few minutes, stirring throughout until you have a lovely thick toffee-like mixture. Pour over the banana. Chill for at least one hour. Before serving, cover completely with the whipped cream.

Strawberry cheesecake
Serves 4–6

If you are an ethical vegetarian you can obtain jelly crystals in health food shops. If you are not so strict you could use a jelly mix (which contains gelatine).

125 g (5 oz) digestives, crushed
70 g (2½ oz) butter
1 sachet vegetarian strawberry jelly crystals
75 ml (3 fl oz) double cream, lightly whipped
250 g strawberry fromage frais
225-g punnet strawberries, halved
2–3 tablespoons (30–45 ml) strawberry jam

Line a 20-cm (8-in) flan tin with foil. Melt the butter in a small pan, add the biscuits and stir well. Press this mixture into the base of the tin and level. Chill. Dissolve the jelly crystals in 125 ml (5 fl oz) boiling water. Then make the jelly up to 200 ml (8 fl oz) with cold water. Leave to cool. When jelly is cool, but not yet beginning to set, mix with the whipped cream and fromage frais and pour on to the biscuit base. Leave to set in the fridge (approximately 1½-2 hours). When filling has set, cover with strawberries. Melt the jam over a gentle heat and spoon over the strawberries. Take out of the tin and remove foil carefully just before serving.

Trifle
Serves 6–8

    8 trifle sponges
    2 tablespoons (30 ml) raspberry jam
    125 ml (5 fl oz) sherry
    20 ratafia biscuits, crushed
    70-g packet instant custard mix
    400-g can mango slices, drained
    1 banana, sliced

To decorate
250-ml carton whipping cream
whole ratafia biscuits
fresh raspberries *or* hundreds and thousands and/*or*
    silver dragées *or* chopped roasted nuts

Split the trifle sponges and sandwich together with the jam. Arrange in a serving bowl and spoon in the sherry. Cover with the crushed ratafia biscuits. Make up the instant custard according to the instructions on the packet. Cool slightly. Add the mango and banana to the trifle and cover with custard. Chill. Whip the cream, spoon over the cold trifle and arrange your chosen decoration on top.

Brown bread and raisin ice-cream
Serves 4

This is utterly delectable, but can be made even naughtier by using Greek yoghurt instead of the low-fat yoghurt I have used in this version. I don't know if you should risk making this if you live in hall, as it must be left in the freezer compartment of the refrigerator and in a communal kitchen this could be risky. It would be tragic to discover that someone else had been unable to resist your delicious dessert! By the way, don't panic about the state of the baking tray when you have cooked the breadcrumbs, just soak it in water and it will clean easily.

2 large slices wholemeal bread, crumbed
6 tablespoons (90 ml) soft brown sugar
140-ml carton whipping cream
300 g low-fat natural yoghurt
50 g (2 oz) raisins

Pre-heat the oven to 200°C/400°F/Gas 6. Mix together the breadcrumbs and sugar and spread over a ba..ing tray. Bake for 10 minutes. Whip the cream until it forms soft peaks, stir in the yoghurt and raisins. Mix in the caramelised breadcrumbs and put into a freezer-proof container. Freeze for 4 hours, then transfer to the fridge for 30 minutes before serving.

Peanut crumblies

Makes 16 biscuits

These are delicious, they just melt in the mouth. You can make them less crumbly by increasing the amount of flour in the mixture to 200 g (8 oz).

> 100 g (4 oz) butter, softened
> 100 g (4 oz) crunchy peanut butter
> 100 g (4 oz) soft brown sugar
> 150 g (6 oz) plain flour

Pre-heat the oven to 190°C/375°F/Gas 5. Cream together the butters and sugar until fluffy. Stir in the flour and mix to a dough using 1–2 teaspoons water to help. Divide into 16, roll into little balls and place these on two non-stick baking trays. Using a dampened fork flatten each ball into a biscuit (but make sure they are not sticking to the trays). Bake for 15–20 minutes. Leave on the trays for 10 minutes before very carefully transferring to a wire rack to cool.

Oat crunchies

Makes 16 biscuits

> 100 g (4 oz) butter, softened
> 50 g (2 oz) soft brown sugar
> 100 g (4 oz) plain flour
> 100 g (4 oz) porridge oats

Pre-heat the oven to 190°C/375°F/Gas 5. Cream together the butter and sugar until fluffy. Mix in the flour and oats, and use your hands to knead into a dough adding 1–2 teaspoons water to help. Divide into 16, roll into little balls and place well apart on two non-stick baking trays. Using a dampened fork, flatten each ball into a biscuit (but make sure they are not sticking to the trays). Bake for 15–20 minutes, until just starting to colour. Transfer carefully to a wire rack to cool.

Flapjacks
Makes 12

    125 g (5 oz) soft margarine
    125 g (5 oz) soft brown sugar
    1 tablespoon (15 ml) golden syrup
    175 g (7 oz) oats

Pre-heat the oven to 190°C/375°F/Gas 5. Melt the margarine, sugar and syrup together. Stir in the oats. Grease a 28 x 18-cm (11 x 7-in) tin and spoon the mixture into it. Press into the base of the tin and level. Bake for about 20 minutes. Mark into portions but leave in the tin to cool. When cold cut out the individual flapjacks.

Muesli flapjacks
Use the above recipe but add an extra tablespoon (15 ml) golden syrup, reduce the amount of oats to 100 g (4 oz) and add 100 g (4 oz) muesli.

Rock cakes
Makes 8–12

You can use wholemeal flour in this recipe but after many years I have reverted to using white as I believe it gives better results.

200 g (8 oz) white flour
1 teaspoon (5 ml) mixed spice
100 g (4 oz) margarine
grated rind of ½ lemon
100 g (4 oz) demerara sugar
100 g (4 oz) mixed dried fruit
1 egg, beaten
1 tablespoon (15 ml) milk
demerara sugar (for sprinkling)

Pre-heat the oven to 200°C/400°F/Gas 6. Rub together the flour, mixed spice and margarine with your fingertips until you have a crumb-like mixture. Stir the other ingredients in thoroughly. Place small dollops of the mixture on a greased baking tray and bake for 15–20 minutes until golden. While still warm, sprinkle with extra demerara sugar.

Strawberry fairy cakes
Makes 12

100 g (4 oz) soft margarine or butter
100 g (4 oz) caster sugar
100 g (4 oz) self-raising flour
2 eggs, beaten

Buttercream
25 g (1 oz) butter, softened
50 g (2 oz) icing sugar
few drops vanilla essence
1–2 teaspoons (5–10 ml) milk
12 small strawberries (to decorate)

Pre-heat the oven to 190°C/375°F/Gas 5. Beat all the cake ingredients together. Spread 12 paper cake cases out on a baking tray and divide the mixture between them. Bake for about 15 minutes until the cakes are golden brown and feel 'springy' when touched. Leave on a wire rack to cool. Then slice off the top of each cake and cut each circle in half making two 'wings'. Make the buttercream by beating the butter, sugar and vanilla essence together, adding just enough milk to form a smooth cream. Put some buttercream on each cake. Top with a strawber y and then place a 'wing' on each side.

Easy fruit cake
Makes 12 portions

This is very easy to make and tastes really good. It keeps well in a cake tin and is a great addition to packed lunches.

150 g (6 oz) soft margarine
150 g (6 oz) muscovado sugar
3 eggs, beaten
200 g (8 oz) plain wholemeal flour
1 teaspoon (5 ml) ground cinnamon
500 g luxury fruit mix
100 g (4 oz) glacé cherries, chopped

Pre-heat the oven to 170°C/325°F/Gas 3. Beat together the margarine and sugar until creamy. Gently beat in the eggs, a little at a time, adding a little flour with the egg to stop the mixture curdling. Then fold in the flour, cinnamon, fruit mix and cherries. Line a 28 x 18-cm (11 x 7-in) baking tin with baking parchment, or greaseproof paper, spoon mixture into tin and level. Cook for 55–65 minutes until risen, brown and firm to the touch. Leave in tin for 5 minutes, then transfer to a wire rack, peel off baking parchment or greaseproof paper and leave to cool.

Passion cake
Serves 8–12

This recipe comes from *Peckish but Poor*. It has proved
incredibly popular – maybe because it scores so highly on
the yummy stakes!

200 g (8 oz) soft margarine
200 g (8 oz) soft brown sugar
4 eggs, beaten
200 g (8 oz) wholemeal self-raising flour
1 teaspoon (5 ml) baking powder
300 g (12 oz) carrots, peeled and grated
grated rind of 1 lemon and 1 tablespoon (15 ml) of
    the juice
100 g (4 oz) chopped walnuts

Icing
75 g (3 oz) cream cheese
50 g (2 oz) icing sugar
grated rind and juice of 1 orange

Pre-heat the oven to 180°C/350°F/Gas 4. Beat together the
margarine, sugar, eggs, flour, baking powder, carrots, lemon
rind and juice and walnuts. Put in a greased and lined 20-cm
(8-in) deep cake tin. Bake for about 90 minutes until well risen
and golden brown. Leave to cool, while you prepare the icing.
Beat together the cream cheese and icing sugar and use just
enough orange juice to achieve a creamy consistency. Cover
the top of the cake with the icing and sprinkle the orange rind
over it.

9 The Slimming Student

This is a tricky topic. With anorexia and bulimia now affecting so many young people, I feel that far too many are trying to lose a few pounds to reach unrealistic weight targets. I definitely belong to the band who would like to see the banning of all fashion advertising and articles which use waif-like models to promote unhealthy images of women. However, as many young people become concerned about their weight at some point, I think it is worth while covering this issue.

The first thing to point out is that if you are maintaining a balanced diet – by this I mean a diet which has a good amount of starchy foods, such as rice, pasta, potatoes and bread, complemented by fresh vegetables and fruit and some proteins, such as beans, nuts and cheese – you will not have many problems with your weight. However, very few people actually stick to this diet. Most of us tend to eat more fats and sugars than we should. And alcohol is very fattening and has no nutritional value.

So if you find yourself putting on a few extra pounds, my advice is to look carefully at your eating habits before

the problem escalates. Are you starting to snack on foodstuffs that are high in either fat or sugar content? If your diet consists of a high proportion of chips, lots of pastry and cheese, crisps and chocolate bars washed down with copious amounts of booze, then you should not be surprised when you start to put on weight! None of these items will hurt if consumed occasionally and in small quantities, but if you want to avoid ballooning you will have to restrict these goodies in your diet. The remedy is obvious: a week or two of a healthy balanced diet, with a ban on the offending goodies and an increase in your exercise regime – you do have an exercise regime don't you? Remember that bodies don't stay young and athletic naturally – should easily do the trick. If you then use a little discretion in the treats you allow yourself each week, you should avoid any further weight problems.

If you are already overweight, following a balanced diet over a few weeks should start to shift those extra pounds (sorry, kilograms!). If this doesn't seem to work, I suggest that a visit to the doctor is in order. Better to be safe than sorry.

I have set out a three-day diet that is easy to follow and will give you an idea of a strict balanced diet. It is not advisable to follow a strict diet for long. You will probably end up bingeing and even heavier than you started. Try this three-day diet and then move on to a normal balanced diet without any treats. This should result in a steady weight loss over a few weeks, then you can slowly start to add some goodies, but only in moderation. I have listed the foods that can be freely eaten on a normal balanced diet and those that should be eaten in moderation or only very occasionally.

3-day diet

Shopping list

6 pieces fruit
450 g (1 lb) new potatoes *or*
   3 x 150 g (6 oz) baking
   potatoes
1 lettuce
1 cucumber
1 courgette
2 onions
200 g (8 oz) mushrooms
2 tomatoes
1 litre (2 pints) skimmed milk
   or 500 ml (1 pint)
   semi-skimmed milk
small carton cottage cheese
   and pineapple
small wholemeal loaf

3 choices from breakfast
   variety packs
250 ml (10 fl oz) vegetable
   soup
200-g can BBQ beans
200-g can baked beans
225-g can pineapple pieces
   in juice
200-g can sweetcorn
200-g can chopped tomatoes
430-g can borlotti beans
oil-free dressing
salt and pepper

Drinks: tea, coffee, water,
   sugar-free drinks

DAY 1

Daily
Milk from allowance
Drinks: tea, coffee, water, sugar-free drinks

Breakfast
variety pack breakfast cereal
milk from allowance

Lunch
vegetable soup
2 slices wholemeal bread
1 piece fruit

Dinner
BBQ beans and pineapple*
green salad made with lettuce, ½ cucumber and ½ grated
    courgette, with oil-free dressing
150 g (6 oz) boiled new potatoes *or* 150 g (6 oz) baked
    potato (see recipe on page 157, but omit margarine)
1 piece fruit

* See page 150.

DAY 2

Breakfast
As Day 1

Lunch
small carton cottage cheese and pineapple
2 slices bread
lettuce
1 piece fruit

Dinner
Bean and pineapple salad*
150 g (5 oz) boiled new potatoes *or* 150 g (6 oz) baked
    potato
1 piece fruit

DAY 3

Breakfast
As other days

Lunch
2 slices toast
200-g can baked beans
1 piece fruit

Dinner
Quick slimmer's stew*
150 g (5 oz) boiled new potatoes *or* 150 g (6 oz) baked
    potato
1 piece fruit

* See pages 150-151.

BBQ beans and pineapple

Serves 1

1 onion, diced
100 g (4 oz) mushrooms, sliced
1 teaspoon (5 ml) oil-free dressing
200-g can BBQ beans
½ 225-g can pineapple pieces, drained, reserving juice

Stir-fry the onion and mushrooms in the oil-free dressing until soft. Add the BBQ beans, the pineapple pieces and 1 tablespoon (15 ml) of the reserved juices. Heat through and serve with potato and salad.

Bean and pineapple salad

Serves 1

½ 430-g can borlotti beans, drained
½ 225-g can pineapple pieces, drained, reserving juice
½ 200-g can sweetcorn
salt and pepper
lettuce
½ cucumber, sliced
½ courgette, grated
2 tomatoes, sliced

Mix together the beans, pineapple and sweetcorn. Add 1 tablespoon (15 ml) of the reserved juices from the pineapple and season well. Arrange the salad ingredients on a plate and top with the bean mixture.

Quick slimmer's stew
Serves 1

    1 onion, diced
    200-g can chopped tomatoes
    200-g can condensed vegetable soup
    100 g (4 oz) button mushrooms
    ½ 430-g can borlotti beans
    ½ 200-g can sweetcorn
    salt and pepper

Pre-heat the oven to 180°C/350°F/Gas 4. In a small pan, bring the onion, tomatoes and soup to the boil, then simmer for 5 minutes. Add the mushrooms and continue cooking for a further 5 minutes. Transfer to a small casserole dish, add the beans and sweetcorn, season and cook for 30 minutes.

A balanced diet

A balanced diet should consist of roughly 30 per cent starchy food, 30 per cent fruit and vegetables, 15 per cent lean protein, 15 per cent dairy products and 10 per cent fats.

Foods that can be eaten freely

Fruit and vegetables
Most fruit and vegetables are low in fat and sugar content. (One exception is the avocado which is high in fat.) Therefore they should play a major part in your diet, preferably fresh, but even frozen or canned. However, remember to buy canned fruit in natural juice, not syrup. Do not add sugar to fruit or fat to vegetables when cooking.

Starchy foods
Examples of starchy foods are cereal, rice, pasta, potatoes. These are another very important group of foods as they add bulk to your meals and ensure that you aren't still hungry at the end of a meal. However, it is very important not to add fat because starchy foods can absorb a lot of it and then become a dieter's enemy.

Foods to be eaten in moderation

Lean proteins
These include beans, pulses and lentils. Although nuts are a good source of protein they are very high in natural oils, so always use sparingly.

Dairy products
This group includes butter, milk, cheese and yoghurt. As these can all be high in fat, you can either use them more sparingly or swap to the lower-fat varieties such as skimmed milk, low-fat cheeses, spreads and yoghurts.

Foods to be eaten only occasionally

Fats
Although we do need some fats in our diet, these are usually provided by the fat content of the other foods we eat. Therefore we need to be very sparing in adding any extra. As well as cutting down the amount of fat we cook with or the dairy products in our diet, we must beware such high fat foods as ice-cream, salad dressings, cakes, biscuits and pastries, chips and crisps, chocolate and many convenience foods.

Example of a day's balanced diet

Breakfast
wholemeal, sugar-free *or* low-sugar cereal with skimmed milk and fresh fruit

Lunch
baked jacket potato with beans and side salad *or*
vegetable soup with wholemeal roll *or*
sandwich made with wholemeal bread with a spicy bean
    filling *or* low-fat cheese, with a side salad *or* plenty of
    salad in the sandwich
piece of fruit

Dinner
Not-so-fattening pasta (see page 154) *or*
    rice *or* potato served with vegetables in sauce. For
    extra protein you could add some beans *or* a small
    amount of nuts to the sauce or serve with grated cheese
a small portion of fruit and natural yoghurt

Not-so-fattening pasta
Serves 1

Contrary to popular belief, you do not have to add fat when you cook and it's not pasta itself that's fattening but what you put on it.

> 200-g can chopped tomatoes
> 1 clove garlic, crushed
> 2 teaspoons (10 ml) tomato purée
> 75 g (3 oz) broccoli florets
> 1 carrot, diced
> 50–75 g (2–3 oz) pasta
> salt and pepper

Put water on to boil for pasta. In a small pan bring the tomatoes, garlic and tomato purée to the boil, then simmer gently for 15 minutes. Over this pan place a steamer or metal colander and steam the broccoli and carrot. Meanwhile, cook the pasta. Drain, place in a bowl, arrange the broccoli and carrots on top and cover with the tomato sauce. Season well.

10 Lifesavers

As term draws to a close, so often does the bank balance! This is the time when you may have to simplify your diet in order to eke out the remaining pennies until the day when you can head for the comforts of home. This is when the staples of student cooking really come into their own. Pasta, rice, potatoes and bread are all cheap and filling. This is the time to start experimenting with them. Search out the items forgotten at the back of your store cupboard – any dried beans, lentils, or cans will come in very useful. With a few extras such as onions, beans and cheese, you will be amazed at what you can produce.

Bean soup
Serves 1–2

> 100 g (4 oz) dried bean mix, soaked overnight
> 1 potato (200 g/8 oz), diced
> 400 ml (16 fl oz) vegetable stock
> 2 onions, 1 chopped, 1 thinly sliced
> 2 cloves garlic, crushed
> 1 tablespoon (15 ml) oil
> knob of butter
> 1 teaspoon (5 ml) brown sugar

Boil the bean mix for 10 minutes, then simmer for about 1 hour until beans are cooked. Cook the potato in the stock for 10 minutes. Fry the chopped onion and garlic in the oil for 5 minutes. Mix the cooked beans and fried onion and garlic in with the potato and stock. Squash some of the beans and potato against the side of the pan to thicken the soup. Simmer for 10 minutes. Meanwhile, fry the sliced onion in the butter and sugar until brown. When soup is ready, sprinkle the browned onion on top and serve.

Baked potatoes
Serves 1

> 1–2 potatoes, cleaned
> knob of margarine
> salt and pepper

Pre-heat the oven to 220°C/425°F/Gas 7. Prick the potatoes all over. Bake for 1–1½ hours (depending on size). Cut in half and fork in margarine. Season well. (Extra cash could buy cheese or baked beans to add as a filling.)

Cheese and Marmite jackets
When the potatoes are cooked, scoop out the flesh, mix with margarine, 1 teaspoon (5 ml) Marmite and 25 g (1 oz) grated cheese. Pre-heat the grill. Put the skins on an ovenproof tray, fill with potato mixture and grill until brown.

Spaghetti
Serve 1

> 100 g (4 oz) wholemeal spaghetti
> knob of margarine
> salt and black pepper
> sprinkling oregano

Cook the spaghetti, drain and add a knob of margarine. Season, sprinkle with oregano and serve. (If finances allow, top with some grated cheese.)

Pasta with tomato and garlic ⊗⊙

Serves 1

This is one of those dishes that I often resort to when my husband Andy is away on one of his trips – travelling the world, visiting all those places I'd love to go to, staying in wonderful hotels, eating and drinking his only relaxation after a hard day's work (oh, not forgetting those business lunches). Well, all I can say is it's a hard life for some! This is an ideal recipe for one as it's extremely quick and simple to make.

> 100 g (400 oz) pasta
> knob of margarine *or* butter
> 1 tablespoon (15 ml) tomato purée
> 1 clove garlic, crushed

Cook pasta in boiling water, then drain. Return to the pan, add the other ingredients and heat through.

Pasta with cheese 'n' herb sauce ⊙

Serves 1

> 75 g (3 oz) pasta
> 1 onion, diced
> 1 tablespoon (15 ml) oil
> 3 tablespoons (45 ml) milk
> 75 g (3 oz) soft cheese, herb and garlic flavoured
> salt and pepper

Cook the pasta in boiling water. Meanwhile, fry the onion in the oil until soft and starting to brown at the edges. Add the milk and cheese and stir, until it melts and makes a sauce. Drain the cooked pasta and mix with the sauce. Season and serve.

Oniony rice ⏱

Serves 1

This is a cheap, simple recipe that is nevertheless very tasty. I love it with tomato sauce.

> 2 onions, 1 chopped, 1 thinly sliced
> 2 tablespoons (30 ml) oil
> 100 g (4 oz) rice
> 375 ml (15 fl oz) vegetable stock
> juice of 1 lemon
> salt and pepper

Fry the chopped onion in 1 tablespoon (15 ml) oil for 5 minutes until soft. Add the rice and stir through. Put in a saucepan with the stock and bring to the boil, then cover and simmer until rice is cooked. Meanwhile, fry the sliced onion in the remaining oil until very brown. When rice is cooked, drain and add lemon juice to taste, season well and serve sprinkled with the browned onion on top.

Rice, potatoes and onions ⏱

Serves 1

Although this is a recipe for when you are utterly broke, don't wait until then to try it. It's really very good. When you're in the money add some mango or lime chutney.

> 200 g (8 oz) potatoes, diced
> oil for frying
> 100 g (4 oz) rice
> 1 onion, sliced
> 1 teaspoon (5 ml) sugar
> soy sauce

Fry the potatoes in the oil while cooking the rice. When the potatoes start to colour, add the onion and continue frying until both are browned. Add the sugar and a dash of soy sauce. (This will make the vegetables slightly sticky as the sugar caramelises.) When the rice is ready, arrange on a plate and pour the caramelised vegetables over it.

11 Round-the-world Veggie Dishes

In this chapter I have tried to keep close to authentic recipes. This may entail purchasing some items that you wouldn't normally buy and you will have to decide if you think it is worthwhile or whether you could substitute something else. All these recipes are goodies that we have picked up on our travels. There are no difficult ones – but there are some very tasty ones! Our particular favourites, which are often cooked in our house, are those for cheese fondue (I'm a fondue fanatic), French onion soup, patatas bravas and pilau rice. However, each one is guaranteed to make an appearance at some time during the year. I hope you have fun trying them out – and that you get to cook some of the recipes in the countries they come from.

Tzatziki ◷
Serves 3–4

200 g Greek yoghurt
¼ cucumber, finely chopped
1 clove garlic, crushed
2 teaspoons (10 ml) white wine vinegar
1 tablespoon (15 ml) fresh mint, chopped

Mix together all the ingredients and serve as a dip or as a sauce for rice dishes.

Simple hummus ◷
Serves 2

This is much better than a shop-bought version. You can make it even creamier by substituting Greek yoghurt for the natural yoghurt. Play around with the amount of garlic and lemon juice that you use to tailor it to your own taste.

420-g can chick peas, drained
1–2 cloves garlic, crushed
juice of ½–1 lemon
2 tablespoons (30 ml) natural yoghurt
1 tablespoon (15 ml) oil

Mash the chick peas until smooth. Add the rest of ingredients and mix well. Serve with toast or pitta bread.

Hummus ☉
Serves 2–4

Tahini is not absolutely essential to this dish but it does add to its authenticity.

> 400-g can chick peas, drained, reserving the liquid
> juice of 1 lemon
> 2 tablespoons (30 ml) tahini
> 2 cloves garlic, crushed
> 1 tablespoon (15 ml) oil

Mash the chick peas to a purée. Gradually add the lemon juice, tahini (if using), garlic, oil and 2 tablespoons (30 ml) of the liquid from the can of chick peas, until you have a thick dip. Chill before serving with toast or pitta bread.

French onion soup
Serves 2

This makes a great meal for two, served with garlic bread and red wine. *Magnifique*!

> 4 onions, sliced thinly
> 75 g (3 oz) butter
> 1 tablespoon (15 ml) plain flour
> 1 clove garlic, crushed
> 2 onion stock cubes
> salt and pepper
> 4 slices French bread
> 50 g (2 oz) cheese, grated

Fry the onions in the butter for 10 minutes until soft and browning. Stir in the flour and garlic, mixing well. Dissolve the stock cubes in 750 ml (1½ pints) boiling water, add to the onion mixture and season. Bring to the boil, then simmer for 20 minutes. Pre-heat the grill. Put the bread on the grill tray, sprinkle with the cheese and grill until it starts to melt. Ladle the soup into bowls and float two slices of bread in each one.

Vichyssoise (potato and leek soup)   ✪⏱

Serves 1–2

This is a useful recipe for a dinner party. If you have access to a blender/liquidiser, you can make it really special by adding a small tub of crème fraîche and liquidising. You will then have a smooth soup which can also be served cold -- with an ice cube or two in the middle and garnished with chopped chives.

> 200 g (8 oz) potatoes, diced
> 200 g (8 oz) leeks, well washed and chopped
> 375 ml (15 fl oz) vegetable stock
> 125 ml (5 fl oz) milk
> salt and pepper

Put all the ingredients in a saucepan and bring to the boil. Cover and simmer for 20 minutes until the vegetables are soft. Check the seasoning and serve.

Greek salad   ⏱

Serves 2

> few crunchy salad leaves
> 2 large tomatoes, sliced
> ½ cucumber, diced
> few slices onion
> 2 tablespoons (30 ml) black olives
> 100 g (4 oz) feta cheese, diced

> *Dressing*
> 2 tablespoons (30 ml) olive oil
> 2 teaspoons (10 ml) wine vinegar
> 1 clove garlic, crushed
> salt and pepper
> squeeze lemon

Put salad ingredients into a bowl. Mix dressing and pour over salad just before serving.

Tabbouleh

Serves 3–4

100 g (4 oz) bulghur wheat
juice from 1 large *or* 2 small lemons
salt and pepper
4 tablespoons (60 ml) olive oil
2 tablespoons (30 ml) parsley, finely chopped
2 tablespoons (30 ml) mint, finely chopped
6 spring onions, sliced
2 tomatoes, peeled and diced

Soak the bulghur wheat in boiling water for 10 minutes. Rinse and drain, squeezing out as much water as possible. Put in a bowl, add the lemon juice and season well. Leave to stand for 20 minutes. Now add the remaining ingredients and stir well.

French dressing

Serves 2–3

3 tablespoons (45 ml) olive oil
1 tablespoon (15 ml) tarragon *or* white wine vinegar
1 teaspoon (5 ml) mustard powder
1 teaspoon (5 ml) caster sugar
1 teaspoon (5 ml) salt
sprinkling black pepper
1 clove garlic, crushed (optional)

Whisk or shake all ingredients together.

Imam bayildi (the priest fainted)
Serves 4–6

A dish that we discovered in Turkey and that I frequently make during the summer months. Serve with lots of crusty French bread to mop up the juices.

1 onion, chopped
2 cloves garlic, crushed
olive oil
1 aubergine, cut into slices lengthways
400-g can chopped tomatoes
2 tablespoons (30 ml) tomato purée
2 tablespoons (30 ml) fresh parsley, chopped

Pre-heat the oven to 180°C/350°F/Gas 4. Fry the onion and garlic in some oil until soft. Put in a casserole dish. Fry the aubergine slices, a few at a time, transferring to the casserole as they brown. (You will need a lot of oil for this.) Then add the remaining ingredients and bake for 45 minutes. Drizzle with more oil before serving. Serve cold.

Patatas bravas
Serves 2

If there is one dish that I absolutely could not live w
is it. I like potato dishes and this one has a heavenly s
are very keen tapas fans, although it's got to be said t   ere
are some pretty ropy imitations of tapas bars around. But there
are also some real gems. Our favourite is in Brighton, Casa
Don Carlos (run by Carlos, of course). His patatas bravas are
great, as is everything on the menu. This is my version.

> 300 g (12 oz) new potatoes, unpeeled
> oil for shallow frying
>
> *Sauce*
> 2 tablespoons (30 ml) olive oil
> 1 tablespoon (15 ml) tomato purée
> 2 teaspoons (10 ml) wine vinegar
> 1 teaspoon (5 ml) paprika
> 1 tablespoon (15 ml) single cream (optional)

Boil the potatoes for 10–15 minutes until just tender but not
soft. Drain and cool, cut into halves or quarters depending on
size. Fry in hot oil until brown. Mix the sauce ingredients
together and pour over potatoes. Serve.

ratin dauphinois ⚙
Serves 4

knob of butter *or* margarine
2 cloves garlic, crushed
1 kg (2 lb) potatoes, sliced very thinly
75 g (3 oz) cheese, grated
salt and pepper
125-ml carton double cream
125 ml (5 fl oz) milk

Pre-heat the oven to 180°C/350°F/Gas 4. Grease a shallow casserole or lasagne dish with the butter or margarine and spread one of the garlic cloves over the bottom. Arrange a layer of potatoes in the dish and sprinkle with one third of the cheese. Season. Repeat the procedure twice. Finally mix together the cream, milk and remaining clove of garlic and pour over the potatoes. Bake for 1 hour or until browned on top.

Refried beans ⚙🕐
Serves 2

400-g can pinto beans, drained
1 onion, chopped
1 clove garlic, crushed
3 tablespoons (45 ml) groundnut oil
salt and pepper
sprinkling chilli powder *or* sauce

Mash beans roughly. Fry the onion and garlic in the oil until soft and golden. Add the beans and stir-fry for 2–3 minutes. Season to taste. Use as an accompaniment for Mexican dishes or to fill burritos or tacos.

Pilau rice
Serves 2–4

We often eat curries in our house, so I keep a number of whole spices in my store cupboard. If you too are a curry fanatic, then I think that it is worthwhile investing in a few spices – they really add an authentic touch to your cooking. This recipe for pilau rice is very popular and better than many of the versions you find in Indian takeaways.

150 g (6 oz) basmati rice, soaked
1 tablespoon (15 ml) oil
½ teaspoon (2.5 ml) whole coriander seeds
½ teaspoon (2.5 ml) whole cumin seeds
½ teaspoon (2.5 ml) whole cardamom seeds
1 teaspoon (5 ml) turmeric
375 ml (15 fl oz) vegetable stock
knob of butter

I like to leave the rice to soak in cold water for 10–15 minutes before using. If this isn't possible, at least put it in a sieve and run plenty of cold water through it. Heat the oil and fry the spices for about one minute, stirring well. Then add the rice, give a good stir and pour in the stock. Stir again, cover with a tight-fitting lid and bring to the boil. Simmer gently for 10–12 minutes until all the stock has been absorbed. Take off the heat, add the butter, cover and leave to stand for 10 minutes before serving.

Spanish tortilla

Serves 2–3

Do pay attention to the fact that for this dish you must have a frying pan that can go under the grill. That is, not only must it fit under the grill but it must have a *heat-proof* handle. If you are the proud possessor of a frying pan with a plastic handle and you try this recipe you will end up with a rather deformed handle! (The time I saw someone fall into this trap it was not even their pan – I don't think the owner ever worked out what had happened.)

    300 g (12 oz) potato, finely cubed
    3 tablespoons (45 ml) oil
    knob of butter
    1 onion, diced
    2 cloves garlic, crushed
    1 red pepper, diced
    4 eggs, beaten
    pinch oregano
    salt and pepper

Fry the potato in the oil until cooked and browned (about 6–8 minutes). Remove the potato from the pan, add the butter and fry the onion, garlic and pepper for 5 minutes. Return the potato to the pan and pour in the eggs which will quickly begin to set. Sprinkle with oregano and season. Cook on a low heat for 2 minutes. Pre-heat the grill. Put the frying pan under the grill and cook until the top of the tortilla is golden brown. Slide on to a plate and cut into wedges. Serve with crusty bread and salad – or unauthentically with baked beans and grilled tomatoes.

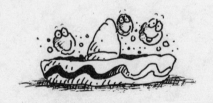

Calzone
Serves 2

If you have never tried these before you are in for a treat. They are a little different from the version my friend Stuart first introduced me to, which merely involved taking one shop-bought pizza, cooking it and then folding it in half and eating it as a sandwich. You could try his way but I think that you will find my way quite a lot tastier. I sometimes substitute a soft garlic and herb flavoured cheese for the ricotta.

> 1 onion, diced
> 1 clove garlic, crushed
> 1 red pepper, finely diced
> 100 g (4 oz) mushrooms, chopped
> 2 tablespoons (30 ml) oil
> 1 packet pizza dough mix
> 2 tablespoons (30 ml) tomato purée
> sprinkling oregano
> 125 g ricotta cheese
> 50 g (2 oz) cheese, grated
> salt and pepper

Pre-heat the oven to 200°C/400°F/Gas 6. Fry the onion, garlic, pepper and mushrooms in the oil until browning. Make up the pizza dough as directed on the packet. Divide into two and flatten each into a 16-cm (6-in) round. Spread them with tomato purée and sprinkle with oregano. Mix the cooked vegetables with the cheeses and divide between the rounds. Season well. Fold each round in half and pinch down the edges, so that you have two pizza pasties. Put on a baking tray and cook for 20–30 minutes until well risen and brown.

Cheese boreks   ⚙ ⏱
Serves 4

We first tried these in Turkey and I was immediately impressed. They are actually very easy to make. Some cookery writers make a big fuss about using filo pastry but I find it very easy to use and don't bother with damp tea towels, etc. Just don't go walkabout in the middle of making these because the pastry will become crisp and unusable if left too long.

> 100 g (4 oz) feta cheese, crumbled
> 1 egg, beaten
> 1 tablespoon (15 ml) fresh chopped mint
> 4 sheets filo pastry
> 25 g (1 oz) melted butter

Pre-heat the oven to 180°C/350°F/Gas 4. Mix together the cheese, egg and mint. Cut each sheet of filo pastry into 3 equal lengths and brush with the melted butter. Place a large teaspoon of mixture at one end of each strip of pastry, roll pastry over filling twice, then fold ends in and continue rolling, so that you have a neat cigar shape with the filling completely enclosed. Put on a greased baking tray and brush with butter. Repeat until you have 12 boreks. Bake for about 15 minutes until crisp and golden.

Burritos (stuffed tortillas)   ⚙ ⏱
Serves 2

> 4 flour tortillas
> refried beans (see page 168)
> 2 tablespoons (30 ml) canned chopped tomatoes
> 50 g (2 oz) cheese, grated

Pre-heat oven to 180°C/350°F/Gas 4. Lay out the tortillas and place a tablespoon of refried beans in the middle of each one. Top with tomatoes and cheese. Fold each tortilla into a parcel, place in an ovenproof dish and cook for 20 minutes. Serve with salsa, sour cream and guacamole (recipes on page 106).

Pistou ✱

Serves 2–4

    1 onion, chopped
    1 clove garlic, crushed
    200 g (8 oz) carrots, diced
    1 green *or* red pepper, diced
    2 tablespoons (30 ml) olive oil
    400-g can chopped tomatoes
    250 ml (10 fl oz) vegetable stock
    50 g (2 oz) small pasta shapes
    1–2 tablespoons (15–30 ml) pesto

Cook onion, garlic, carrots and pepper in oil until soft. Add the tomatoes and stock and bring to the boil. Cover and simmer for 15 minutes. Add the pasta shapes and cook for a further 10 minutes. Stir in the pesto and serve with crusty French bread.

Cheese fondue ✱ ◷

Serves 4

This is still popular in our house – though not so much with Andy. Unfortunately he broke the fondue pot I had bought in Switzerland and I'm insisting that I need another trip there to replace it!

    300 ml (12 fl oz) dry white wine
    400 g (1 lb) Cheddar, grated
    200 g (8 oz) gruyère *or* emmental, grated
    miniature of vodka *or* gin
    4 teaspoons (20 ml) cornflour
    large fresh baguette, cut into big chunks

Heat the wine in a large saucepan. Add the cheeses. Cook for a few minutes, stirring constantly, until cheeses melt. Dissolve the cornflour in the vodka or gin and add to the mixture, continuing to stir until the fondue thickens. Serve in bowls with chunks of crusty bread to dip.

Spiced couscous ⊕
Serves 4

This is quite a spicy dish; the cinnamon gives it a very unusual taste.

> 1 aubergine (200 g/8 oz), cubed
> 1 potato (200 g/8 oz), cut into matchsticks
> 200 g (8 oz) carrots, sliced
> 375 ml (15 fl oz) vegetable stock
> 1 onion, sliced
> 1 pepper, diced
> 4 cloves garlic, crushed
> 2 tablespoons (30 ml) oil
> 1 teaspoon (5 ml) chilli powder
> 1 teaspoon (5 ml) cinnamon
> 1 teaspoon (5 ml) ground ginger
> 400-g can chopped tomatoes
> 200 g (8 oz) couscous
> 50 g (2 oz) butter
> 100 g (4 oz) raisins
> 50 g (2 oz) toasted almonds

Put the aubergine, potato, carrots and stock in a saucepan, bring to the boil, then cover and simmer for 20 minutes until vegetables are tender. Meanwhile, fry the onion, pepper and garlic in the oil until soft. Add the spices, stir-fry for 1 minute, pour in the tomatoes and simmer for 10 minutes. Cook the couscous as directed on the packet and mix with the butter, raisins and almonds. Strain the boiled vegetables and add to the tomato mixture. Serve the couscous with the vegetables over the top.

Veggie bobotie
Serves 4

Since the changes in South Africa, Andy has found hims⌐
frequent visitor to that beautiful country. He has even b⌐
lucky enough to be invited to stay in a private house instead of
always having to stay in hotels. The cuisine is something that
he has been very impressed with. This is my version of one of
their national dishes.

1 onion, chopped
1 clove garlic, crushed
1 tablespoon (15 ml) oil
1 tablespoon (15 ml) medium curry paste
400 g Vegemince
1 large slice wholemeal bread, soaked in 3 tablespoons
    (45 ml) water
8 ready to eat apricots, chopped
2 large bananas
salt and pepper
2 eggs, beaten
250 ml (10 fl oz) milk
pinch turmeric

Pre-heat the oven to 180°C/350°F/Gas 4. Fry the onion and
garlic in the oil until soft, add the curry paste and cook for
2 minutes. Add the Vegemince and 375 ml (15 fl oz) water
and simmer for 5 minutes. Mash the bread and stir in, together
with the apricots. Mash one banana and add to the mixture.
Season. Transfer to an ovenproof dish. Cover and bake for 20
minutes. Beat the eggs, milk and turmeric together. Remove
dish from the oven, uncover and pour in egg mixture. Slice
the remaining banana lengthways and arrange over the top.
Bake, uncovered, for another 30 minutes until the top is firm
and golden. Serve hot.

Index

A selection of non-fiction from Headline

THE DRACULA SYNDROME	Richard Monaco & William Burt	£5.99	☐
PROCLAIMED IN BLOOD	Hugh Miller	£5.99	☐
MURDER BOOK OF DAYS	Brian Lane	£6.99	☐
THE MURDER YEARBOOK 1995	Brian Lane	£5.99	☐
THE PLAYFAIR CRICKET ANNUAL	Bill Findall	£3.99	☐
KEITH: TILL I ROLL OVER DEAD	Stanley Booth	£5.99	☐
THE JACK THE RIPPER A–Z	Paul Begg, Martin Fido & Keith Skinner	£7.99	☐
THE *DAILY EXPRESS* HOW TO WIN ON THE HORSES	Danny Hall	£5.99	☐
AT HOME WITH FRED	Rupert Fawcett	£5.99	☐
GRAPEVINE; THE COMPLETE WINEBUYER'S HANDBOOK	Anthony Rose & Tim Atkin	£6.99	☐
THE LEX FAMILY WELCOME GUIDE TO HOTELS, PUBS AND RESTAURANTS	Jill Foster & Malcolm Hamer	£7.99	☐

All Headline books are available at your local bookshop or newsagent, or can be ordered direct from the publisher. Just tick the titles you want and fill in the form below. Prices and availability subject to change without notice.

Headline Book Publishing, Cash Sales Department, Bookpoint, 39 Milton Park, Abingdon, OXON, OX14 4TD, UK. If you have a credit card you may order by telephone – 01235 400400.

Please enclose a cheque or postal order made payable to Bookpoint Ltd to the value of the cover price and allow the following for postage and packing:

UK & BFPO: £1.00 for the first book, 50p for the second book and 30p for each additional book ordered up to a maximum charge of £3.00.
OVERSEAS & EIRE: £2.00 for the first book, £1.00 for the second book and 50p for each additional book.

Name ....

Address ....

....

....

If you would prefer to pay by credit card, please complete:
Please debit my Visa/Access/Diner's Card/American Express (delete as applicable) card no:

Signature .... Expiry Date ....